T0146439

TEN REASONS WHY JESUS IS COMING SOON

10

REASONS WHY JESUS IS COMING SOON

Ten Christian Leaders Share Their Insights

Multnomah Books *Sisters, Oregon*

TEN REASONS WHY JESUS IS COMING SOON
published by Multnomah Publishers, Inc.

©1998 by Multnomah Publishers, Inc.
International Standard Book Number: 9781590528808

For information:
MULTNOMAH PUBLISHERS, INC.•POST OFFICE BOX 1720
SISTERS, OREGON 97759

146651086

CONTENTS

INTRODUCTION

Of all of the major religions of the world, only Christianity gives real hope for the future. While most people are concerned about the future, they wonder where to turn for answers. Astrologists? Futurologists? Gurus? Evening News? Books? Preachers? Only the Bible gives accurate prophesies—yet we know so little about them when so much is available!

At the core of biblical prophecy is the prediction of the Second Coming of Jesus Christ. He literally came the first time as a babe in Bethlehem as was predicted. For every prophecy telling of the first coming there are scores announcing His Second Coming.

This book features ten of today's great Bible teachers who provide answers about the future.

"The Lord is going to return. We need to get ready," says Chuck Swindoll.

"The signs of insecurity and shouts of revelation heard around the world are perhaps the death rattle of an era in civilization.… The Scriptures promise that He (God) will act dramatically. He will send His Son back to earth." Billy Graham.

"The hour hand on God's time clock is wound up and spinning." David Jeremiah.

These are biblical specialists. Not only do they all believe that Jesus is coming again but there is overwhelming evidence that He could come any day.

Let me warn you though, the contents of this book will challenge your life. It will affect how you think, plan, and prioritize.

So if you've been concerned about crime, greed, El Nino,

economic crisis, human rights, famine, disease or the future of your children and grandchildren, this book will let you in on a major secret—you and your family can be ready for His Coming.

So with the words of Jesus himself, "Yes, I am coming *soon*" we echo with John the Apostle "Amen. Come Lord Jesus" (Revelation 22:20).

John Van Diest

GENERAL EDITOR

THE SCRIPTURES ANTICIPATE HIS COMING

CHARLES R. SWINDOLL

Charles R. Swindoll, D.D.
President, Dallas Theological Seminary
President, Insight for Living radio ministry
Author of nine Gold Medallion books

The return of Jesus Christ never fails to create mixed emotions. For those who are ready for it, there is always a sense of comfort and anticipation. A feeling not unlike the Delta Airlines motto— "We're ready when you are." For those who are not ready for it (or do not believe in it), there is a mixture of responses. Some are irritated. Some are intimidated. A few are afraid, maybe a little panicked. Most simply refuse to think about it. But no one can remain neutral on the subject.

Those thoughts remind me of the true story of what happened to a friend of mine many years ago before he became a Christian. He was hitchhiking his way across the United States. Around dusk one evening, when it looked like rain, he was hoping for a car to pull over before the showers began to fall. Sure enough, a car swerved over to his side of the road, the door flew open, and he heard the driver say, "Hop in." So my friend hopped in, slammed the door, and they took off just as the rain started to fall.

Although daylight was rapidly fading, my friend could just make out the words on a small poster that had been stuck to the dashboard—

WARNING, IN THE EVENT OF CHRIST'S RETURN
THIS DRIVER WILL DISAPPEAR;
THIS CAR WILL SELF-DESTRUCT

Then in bold, red letters, four final words:

YOU BETTER GIT READY

Years later as he was relating the story to me, I asked him how he felt that eerie evening when he read those words. Smiling, he said, "Well, as a matter of fact, it was spooky! I didn't know whether to write my will, to pray, or to jump. But I remember doing two things. First, I kept my door unlocked (as if that were going to help); and second, I engaged the driver in nonstop conversation. I figured he wouldn't suddenly disappear if we kept on talking together."

Isn't it funny how superstitious people can be about future things? And isn't it amazing what decisions people make, thinking that "somehow things will just work out" if they stay close to the right people? It calls to mind the lady who wanted to marry four different men in her lifetime. She said each one would help her with the four things she needed most. First, she wanted to marry a banker. Second, a movie star. Next, a clergyman. And finally, a funeral director. When asked why, she answered, "One for the money, two for the show, three to get ready, and four to go!"

Back to my original story. The driver of the car considered Christ's coming a solid comfort, but the rider viewed it as something spooky…a fearful thought. Again, it is almost impossible to remain neutral regarding this future event.

EXTREMES THAT BLOCK OUR BALANCE

Fanatical Intensity

Some Christians drop straight off the deep end when prophetic subjects come up. They almost "go nuts" over the subject. When that happens, they seem to lose their practical equilibrium. Such fanatical intensity invariably drives others away as these well-meaning folks overreact to the teaching of prophecy.

Some of the telltale signs? They begin to read prophecy into most newspaper articles, current events, and certainly each major disaster or calamity. They are often surprised that you don't see it as clearly as they do. What's worse, their neurotic intensity creates within them a lack of interest in the here and now. Nothing— absolutely nothing—is more important to them than the then and there. Often, they tend to live rather sheltered and/or irresponsible lives. Some don't mind increasing their indebtedness. After all, their soon departure from Planet Earth provides the perfect escape from financial responsibility! They don't worry too much about today's assignments, either, because they are so caught up in the tomorrow of God's plan.

The ultimate extremists would be those who set specific dates, then quit their jobs and mooch off others as they wait for the Lord's return.

Many years ago I found a big tract stuck under the windshield wiper on my car. I remember it well. It was one of those four-page, tiny-print jobs. Almost needed a magnifying glass to read the stuff. I can't recall how may dozens of points there were that this person (who happened to be a member of a religious cult) tried to communicate. But his logic was strange and the verses he quoted were twisted and wrenched from their context.

What caught my eye was the date that was set...January 31, 1974! Some kind of comet with a blazing tail of fire would bring a "baptism of fire" that would cause a wave of insanity and suicide throughout the earth shortly before Christ returned...and we wouldn't be able to escape it if we remained in the United States. We in America needed to be prepared by moving to Canada or Mexico or Puerto Rico or even Hawaii. (It's always safer in Hawaii, it seems.) Everything was sure to end January 31, 1974. Well, on February 1, 1974, I wrote to the address that appeared on the bottom of the tract. I asked a few pointed questions, but I never got an answer. Maybe they were all in Hawaii by then.

Frankly, I call that sort of stuff "prophecy gone to seed." Too much prophetic intensity gets dangerously close to personal insanity.

No matter how much we may love the Lord Jesus Christ and believe in His Word, we need to remember that there is still a life to be lived and responsibilities to be faced. And to cop out because Christ is coming is not only poor practicality, it's abominable theology. Never once in Scripture is irresponsibility excused on the basis of one's confidence in Christ's return. Anticipation is one thing. Blind fanaticism is quite another.

Theological Ignorance

The other extreme to the far left is theological ignorance. Maybe "personal indifference" would be another way of putting it. The former problem is one of being over-involved and super-intense. But the indifferent individual sees no reason at all to be alert. In fact, he seriously questions that there will even be such a thing as a Second Coming. A person like that has no interest in evangelism (I have never seen an exception), because there is an absence of urgency. He understands neither God's overall world program nor specifically the imminent (at-any-moment) return of Christ.

There's something about Christ's soon return that stirs up our urgency and keeps us involved. God planned it that way. Anticipating the Savior activates our involvement in today's needs.

C. S. Lewis writes:

Hope is one of the theological virtues. This means that a continual looking forward to the eternal world is not (as some modern people think) a form of escapism or wishful thinking, but one of the things a Christian is meant to do. It does not mean that we are to leave the present world as it is. If you read history, you will find that the Christians who did most for the present world were just those who thought most of the next...It is since Christians have largely ceased to think of the other world that they have become so ineffective in this. Aim at heaven and you will get earth "thrown in": aim at earth and you will get neither.[1]

Needed Balance

Let's be neither insane nor indifferent about His return. What we need is a balance. We need to be informed and aware, thinking it could occur at any moment, but carrying out our lives as responsibly as if His return would not be for another two or three generations.

In other chapters we have examined Peter's words. Let's look again, this time at his second letter. In this section he writes as an eyewitness of the Lord Jesus. He is building to a climax: the return of the Lord.

> For we did not follow cleverly devised tales when we made known to you the power and coming of our Lord Jesus Christ, but we were eyewitnesses of His majesty. For when He received honor and glory from God the Father, such an utterance as this was made to Him by the Majestic Glory, "This is My beloved Son with whom I am well pleased"—and we ourselves heard this utterance made from heaven when we were with Him on the holy mountain. And so we have the prophetic word made more sure, to which you do well to pay attention as a lamp shining in a dark place, until the day dawns and the morning star arises in your hearts (2 Peter 1:16–19).

Is that a relevant word? You bet! "I have seen Him. I have heard the voice from heaven. I have listened to His teachings with my own ears and we have a more sure word. You'd do well to listen up."

Next, glance at chapter 3, verses 3 and 4. He writes perhaps to skeptical ears as he says:

> Know this first of all, that in the last days mockers will come with their mocking, following after their own lusts, and saying, "Where is the promise of His coming? For ever since the fathers fell asleep, all continues just as it was from the beginning of creation.

Does that sound like something you heard in your science classes? Did they teach you that in your undergraduate or graduate studies? Probably so. It's called the theory of uniformitarianism. Since the beginning of time to this present day there has been the unfolding, the evolving, of an *uninterrupted* flow of events in history.

"Wrong," says Peter. "They were wrong. They systematically overlook something that intercepted time—the deluge, the universal flood."

> For when they maintain this, it escapes their notice that by the word of God the heavens existed long ago and the earth was formed out of water and by water, through which the world at that time was destroyed, being flooded with water (vv. 5–6).

"They overlook a very important fact," says Peter. "They forget that this earth, as it was created by God and as history was unfolding, was destroyed. They ignore the fact that in the middle of the movement of time, God stepped in and brought a flood. And it caught the attention of everyone on this earth—this deluge." To this day most scholars overlook (or, in some cases explain away) the possibility of a universal flood.

Suddenly, Peter jumps to the future.

> But the present heavens and earth by His word are being reserved for fire,...(v. 7a).

Before, it was destroyed by water. Someday in the future it will be destroyed by fire.

...kept for the day of judgment and destruction of ungodly men. But do not let this one fact escape your notice, beloved, that with the Lord one day is as a thousand years, and a thousand years as one day. The Lord is not slow about His promise, as some count slowness, but is patient toward you, not wishing for any to perish but for all to come to repentance (vv. 7b–9).

The Lord is going to return. We need to "git ready." He doesn't wish for any to perish. I call that clear, specific, and reliable information. When it comes to balance, that says it well. Let's not mistake our Lord's current patience for permanent absence. He *is* coming back.

PREDICTIONS THAT AFFIRM OUR ASSURANCE

Before looking at other verses of Scripture, let me take you on a brief safari. To begin with, here are some facts about prophecy that will surprise most people:

- One out of every 30 verses in the Bible mentions the subject of Christ's return or the end of time.
- Of the 216 chapters in the New Testament, there are well over 300 references to the return of Jesus Christ.
- Only 4 of the 27 New Testament books fail to mention Christ's return.
- That means one-twentieth of the entire New Testament is dedicated to the subject of our Lord's return.
- In the Old Testament, such well-known and reliable men of God as Job, Moses, David, Isaiah, Jeremiah, Daniel, and most of the minor prophets, fixed at least part of their attention on the Lord's return.

- Christ spoke of His return often, especially after He had revealed His death. He never did so in vague or uncertain terms.
- Those who lived on following His teaching, who established the churches and wrote the Scriptures in the first century, frequently mentioned His return in their preaching and in their writings.

After those apostles left the earth, that message of Christ's return did not die. On the contrary, it found its way into the Nicene Creed, into the Athanasian Creed, and into the thirty-nine Articles of the Church of England, the fourth of which says, "He ascended into heaven and there sitteth until He returns to judge all men at the last day." The Augsburg Confession deals with it somewhat at length. The familiar Apostle's Creed, repeated at many churches in their liturgy of worship, includes the statement, "from thence He shall come to judge the quick and the dead."

I remember repeating those words as a little boy in a church where our family worshipped. I wondered who "the quick" would be at that time. I understood "the dead." I didn't grasp that *quick* is the Old English term for "living." "He will come to judge the living and the dead."

The Bible teaches it. The Lord Jesus stood upon its truths. The apostles declared it and wrote about it. The creeds include it and affirm it. Quite obviously, His return has not been considered an insignificant issue through the centuries. But the strange thing is that many Christians in this generation either ignore it or are somehow confused by it. Too bad. It is a marvelous truth that only gains significance as we move closer to death.

A few days ago I had a part in the burial of a twenty-one-year-old man who died in an automobile accident. It was a heartrending service. I thought of Christ's return as I looked at the casket. The thought gave me reassuring hope. Only a few days later, one of our long-time church "saints," a godly, one-hundred-year-old woman, passed into the Lord's presence. And when I heard that news, immediately thoughts of Jesus' return flashed through my mind:

> For the Lord Himself will descend from heaven with a shout, with the voice of the archangel, and with the trumpet of God; and the dead in Christ shall rise first. Then we who are alive and remain shall be caught up together with them in the clouds to meet the Lord in the air, and thus we shall always be with the Lord (1 Thessalonians 4:16–17).

Whether young or old, those who pass into eternity have the same truth to claim…and so do those of us who remain. It is something you can cling to when it seems as though all hell has broken loose in your life. When the events of your days seem out of control, having neither rhyme nor reason. Deep within you are reminded that the end has not yet come. When He comes it will all make sense.

Let's take a moment to look briefly at several verses of Scripture that underscore His soon coming.

Matthew 24 is a great place to start. Jesus is speaking:

> Therefore be on the alert, for you do not know which day your Lord is coming. But be sure of this, that if the head of the house had known at what time of the night the thief

was coming, he would have been on the alert and would not have allowed his house to be broken into. For this reason you be ready too; for the Son of Man is coming at an hour when you do not think He will (vv. 35–38).

But when the Son of Man comes in His glory, and all the angels with Him, then He will sit on His glorious throne (25:31).

Notice the words "when" and "will"—not "if," but "when"… not "may," but "will." There was no question in Jesus' mind.

From Matthew 25, turn to Mark, chapter 8.

For whoever wishes to save his life shall lose it; and whoever loses his life for My sake and the gospel's shall save it. For what does it profit a man to gain the whole world, and forfeit his soul? For what shall a man give in exchange for his soul? For whoever is ashamed of Me and My words in this adulterous and sinful generation, the Son of Man will also be ashamed of him when He comes in the glory of His Father with the holy angels" (vv. 35–38).

This kind of teaching must have stunned the disciples. They had anticipated the establishment of Jesus' earthly kingdom then and there. They expected it to be in motion before the end of their generation, when Jesus would be ruling as King of kings and Lord of lords. They envisioned themselves as charter members in His kingdom band. With great delight they would witness the overthrow of Rome and Israel's numerous enemies. What a hope!

But then one dark night in a second-story flat, along some street in the city of Jerusalem, Jesus ate His last meal with them.

There, He unfolded the startling truth that His death was only hours away. They must have wanted to stop their ears from hearing Him say, "I'm going to leave you. I'm going back to My Father."

Looking into the eyes of those disillusioned men who must have felt a bit orphaned, Jesus said:

> Let not your heart be troubled; believe in God, believe also in Me. In My Father's house are many dwelling places; if it were not so, I would have told you; for I go to prepare a place for you (John 14:1–2).

It is very important that you understand heaven, our eternal destiny is an *actual place*. It isn't a misty dream or a floating fantasy. Don't let any of the mystical religions confuse you. Heaven is reality. Literal real estate which He is preparing for His own. Jesus says so in the next statement.

> And if I go and prepare a place for you, I will come again, and receive you to Myself; that where I am, there you may be also (v. 3).

The body of every believer that now resides in a casket, every believer torn apart by ravenous beasts, or by the elements of the sea, or by warfare, or awful murder will be received by Christ at His return. Regardless of the condition of that body, the Lord Jesus says, "I *will* come again, and I *will* receive you unto Myself." That's a direct promise from His lips. Most of those men who heard His words that evening died horrible deaths. More than one of them were sawn in two. Some were torn apart by wild beasts. Yet their

Lord said, in effect, "I will come again, and I'll receive you unto Myself. The condition of your body doesn't concern Me. This promise stands firm"

Shortly thereafter Jesus went to the cross. When He died He was placed in a tomb. Three days later, He emerged in bodily form from the tomb, victorious over death. He is the only one thus far who has ever been resurrected—the only one to come back to this earth in a glorified condition. So He has overcome death. In light of that, it shouldn't surprise us that He is able to bring us from the grave when He returns.

Forty days after His resurrection He stood on a mountain with His followers. While there, just before He ascended to heaven, the same subject was brought up again—His return.

> And so when they had come together, they were asking Him, saying, "Lord, is it at this time You are restoring the kingdom to Israel?" He said to them, "It is not for you to know times or epochs which the Father has fixed by His own authority; but you shall receive power when the Holy Spirit has come upon you, and you shall be My witnesses both in Jerusalem, and in all Judea and Samaria, and even to the remotest part of the earth." And after He had said these things, He was lifted up while they were looking on, and a cloud received Him out of their sight (Acts 1:6–9).

Wow! Can you *imagine* that moment? As they watched, Jesus was lifted up out of sight. We think we're pretty hot stuff because we can put people in a rocket and send them into an orbit around the earth a few times, then bring them back. Yet with no physical assistance, with nothing around Him or near Him, He was lifted up from the earth—whoosh!—and went directly through the clouds back to heaven. His followers did just what you and I would have done—they stood with mouths open, gazing intently into the skies.

> And as they were gazing intently into the sky while He was departing, behold, two men in white clothing stood beside them; and they also said, "Men of Galilee,…(v. 10–11a).

I want to write the following words to people who are preoccupied with Christ's return, spending most of their time looking up, as if they had nothing else to do—

> …"Men of Galilee, why do you stand looking into the sky? This Jesus, who has been taken up from you into heaven, will come in just the same way as you have watched Him go into heaven."

He is coming back. Looking up won't bring Him any sooner. We're never told simply to stand around gazing up to heaven. In fact, we're told *not* to do that. We aren't even commanded to do a lot of talking about it. There's a bigger job to be done than sitting around discussing the details of His return!

In the last book of the Bible, Revelation, Jesus is being quoted by John who writes these last words:

> I, Jesus, have sent My angel to testify to you these things for the churches. I am the root and the offspring of David, the bright morning star…He who testifies to these things

says, "Yes, I am coming quickly." Amen. Come, Lord Jesus (22:16–20).

SCRIPTURES THAT DESCRIBE OUR DESTINY

So much for a general overview. There are two passages that are worth turning back to and getting a little closer focus on. First Corinthians 15:50–58 is the first and 1 Thessalonians 4:13–18 is the second. Both of these scriptures describe our destiny. The Corinthian passage emphasizes the *changes* that will come over us when Christ returns for His own. The Thessalonian passage emphasizes the *order of events* that will occur in the future.

First Corinthians 15:50–58

After developing a thorough statement on resurrection, the apostle Paul presents a transition in verse 50.

> Now I say this, brethren, that flesh and blood cannot inherit the kingdom of God; nor does the perishable inherit the imperishable.

Understand what he means. He is talking to those of us who are earthlings, people who have been earthbound all our lives. We are people in the process of dying. How many of us in our fifties can remember our younger days when we were in our twenties? We felt differently and we certainly looked differently. Now there are physical signs on our bodies that mark us as aging people. We all have loved ones in their seventies and eighties, maybe even their nineties, who certainly reveal "perishable" mortality. In order for these bodies of ours to last throughout eternity in what is here called "the kingdom of God," *there must be a change* so that our bodies are made ageless. There must be some kind of molecular reconstruction within us that prepares us for eternity. Our bodies must be changed into a glorified state. All these changes will equip our bodies to last eternally. Since our future will be a bodily existence in heaven, we must undergo bodily changes. Remember now, our eternal existence is not simply spirit existence, but bodily existence. So Paul emphasizes our future changes in the next three verses:

> Behold, I tell you a mystery; we shall not all sleep, but we shall all be changed, in a moment, in the twinkling of an eye, at the last trumpet; for the trumpet will sound, and the dead will be raised imperishable, and we shall be changed. For this perishable must put on the imperishable, and this mortal must put on immortality (vv. 51–53, emphasis mine).

Paul calls this revelation "a mystery." In our day a *mystery* suggests something that is complicated, like a riddle, hard to unravel and difficult to solve...complex. But a mystery in Paul's day (*Musterion*) was not something that was complex, but something that was more like our word "secret." It's like he was writing, "Listen, I want to tell you a secret." There's a difference. Once someone tells you a secret, it isn't complicated. All you need is the information.

Here's the thought: "Behold, I want to reveal something that has been a secret up to now...something you will find mentioned nowhere else in God's revelation prior to this revelation." What is that secret? Namely this: There will be a generation alive at the time Christ comes back...and those living believers at the time Christ returns, will be instantly changed and taken back to be with Him forever. Not only will the dead be raised and changed, but those believers who are alive will also be changed.

But when this perishable will have put on the imperishable, and this mortal will have put on immortality, then will come about the saying that is written, "Death is swallowed up in victory. O death, where is your victory? O death, where is your sting?" (vv. 54–55).

Paul didn't get that from Shakespeare; Shakespeare got that from Paul! Death will have won its final victory. When we are taken up, the grim reaper will hang up his scythe. Finally, at long last, Death will bite the dust. Up to now it may seem he is king. Death visits every home. He steps into the life of every person who has ever lived. No matter how great or how cruel, how good or how bad, death comes. And as he is often pictured, the grim reaper cuts everyone down to size. Euripedes the poet was right, "Death is the debt we all must pay." But the marvelous good news is that when our final change at Christ's coming occurs, death will never again have charge of us. At that glorious moment we shall begin a timeless, ageless existence. For the next few moments, meditate on the closing words in this chapter.

The sting of death is sin, and the power of sin is the law; but thanks be to God, who gives us the victory through our Lord Jesus Christ. Therefore, my beloved brethren, be steadfast, immovable, always abounding in the work of the Lord, knowing that your toil is not in vain in the Lord (1 Corinthians 15:56–58).

How often I quote these words to myself!

First Thessalonians 4:13–18

Remember now, we have nothing to worry about regarding the condition of the body when death occurs. *We shall be changed.* The

One who made our bodies from nothing will have no difficulty making us again, even from little bits and pieces if necessary. He'll be able to put us all together.

Let me point out four observations from this passage.

1. We are to be informed.

> But we do not want you to be uninformed, brethren,
> about those who are asleep…(v. 13a).

As I have said all along, ignorance is not bliss. The Lord doesn't smile on us when, as we think about the future, we say, "Well, actually, nobody can know for sure. We just hope things work out all right." That's an ignorant and incorrect response. He *wants* us to be informed and knowledgeable. We are to know what's in front of us—at least the broad brush strokes of His plan. Knowing the future gives us confidence in the present.

2. We are not to grieve as those without hope.

> But we do not want you to be uninformed, brethren,
> about those who are asleep, that you may not grieve, as
> do the rest who have no hope (v. 13).

Death brings sorrow. Sorrow brings tears. Tears are part of the grieving process. God never tells us, "Don't cry. Don't grieve." He says we are not to grieve *as those who have no hope.* I am saddened when I see parents, well-meaning though they may be, who correct their children for crying because a loved one dies. Crying is the most natural response when we lose someone or something important to us. We have every reason to grieve and to be sad, but our grief is not as the hopeless when they grieve. You see, we have an answer beyond the grave. They do not. It is this hope that ultimately brings comfort.

THE SCRIPTURES ANTICIPATE HIS COMING

3. We are to face death without fear.

> For if we believe that Jesus died and rose again, even so
> God will bring with Him those who have fallen asleep in
> Jesus (1 Thessalonians 4:14).

Now the reason Christ's own resurrection is so important is
because we can anticipate rising as He did. Had He not come back
from beyond, we couldn't expect to either. I often think of the followers of some guru. They die. They look next to them in the
grave and—there's their guru! Their great spiritual leader. He's still
there. If he didn't get out himself, then I ask you how is he going
to get *them* out? But no one will ever see a dead Jesus. Why? He
has been raised. He has gone beyond the grave. His tomb is
empty. Because He died and rose again He is able to give us an
answer to sin, death, and the grave. If we believe in Him, then we
are ready to be taken with Him. He will bring us along with all
those who have fallen asleep in Jesus. Because He lives, all fear is
gone!

4. We're to know the order of events.

> For this we say to you by the word of the Lord, that we
> who are alive, and remain until the coming of the Lord,
> shall not precede those who have fallen asleep. For the
> Lord Himself will descend from heaven with a shout,
> with the voice of the archangel, and with the trumpet of
> God; and the dead in Christ shall rise first. Then we who
> are alive and remain shall be caught up together with
> them in the clouds to meet the Lord in the air, and thus
> we shall always be with the Lord (vv. 15–17).

Here is the overall order of events: "The Lord Himself will descend
from heaven." That's *first.* I like the way Phillips renders it:

One word of command, one shout from the archangel,
one blast from the trumpet of God…

Imagine the scene! Perhaps all those things will come simultaneously…in one great voice, one grand sound. I smile as I write
these words. They never fail to excite me!

Next, "the dead in Christ shall rise first."

Then, "we who are alive and remain shall be caught up
together with the…"

With whom? The dead who have been changed, who have
been raised ahead of us.

Finally, we—

…shall be caught up together with them in the clouds to
meet the Lord in the air, and thus we shall always be with
the Lord (v. 17b).

It is my personal conviction that our Lord Jesus will come for
us in the sky—in the clouds. Following that reunion in the air,
there will occur on this earth a time of awful judgment, a time of
unrestrained pain and great tribulation, following which our
savior will return to this earth and establish the fulfillment of His
millennial promises to Israel, a literal one-thousand-year reign
over this earth as He serves as King of kings and Lord of lords. My
personal believe is that the return of the Lord Jesus for His own,
as described in Thessalonians and in Corinthians, is *prior* to His
establishment of a literal kingdom on earth over which He reigns
as King.

This pegs me as a pretribulational premillenialist! But don't let
all that make you nervous. I still have great fellowship with those
in other camps. Not everybody does, however. I heard about a

guy who was so premillennial he wouldn't even eat Post Toasties!

Now the most important thing for you to understand is that *He is coming again.* And, secondly that *it is a comfort to you* because you have believed in Him. Be sure that the one you believe in has conquered death, otherwise he won't get you into heaven. Hell awaits you. The only way to get beyond the grave and into the Lord's presence is to place your trust on One who has gone before you and has paved the way.

ACTIONS THAT REVEAL OUR READINESS

I think there are at least three ways we reveal our readiness.

First, we continue to walk by faith. Rather than walking by sight and shaping our lives on the basis of the visible, we walk by faith.

Second, we continue to live in peace. We view the present and our future not with panic but with peace. We don't live worried, hassled lives.

And *third,* we rely on hope. The hope that gets me through the tests on this earth is the same hope that gets me through the grave at death, because the One in whom I have believed has gone before me. He is preparing a place for me. He is the embodiment of my hope. Because He lives, we shall live also. The secret of escape from the prison of this body and the pain of this planet is knowing the One who can guarantee our getting beyond the grave.

A recent "Alfred Hitchcock" TV episode showed the flip side to this sure and certain hope. As you might expect, the point was made in a rather chilling way.

There was this rather wicked, two-faced woman who mur-dered an individual. And though she had often done wrong on previous occasions and had always gotten away with it, the court found her guilty in this case and the judge sentenced her to life in prison. Even though she screamed in the judge's face and announced that she would escape from any prison they put her into, they sent her away.

She took that infamous bus ride to the prison. En route, she noticed something that became part of her escape plan. She saw an old man, an inmate, covering up a grave outside the prison walls. She realized the only way to get out of prison was to know someone who had the key to the gate. The only one who did was the old man who assisted in the burial of those who died within the walls. Actually, he built the caskets as well as placed the remains in each casket. His job included rolling the casket on an old cart to the gravesite outside the wall and then lowering it into the hole and covering it up with dirt.

The old man was going blind. He needed cataract surgery, but he had no money to pay for it. She told him that it would be worth his while if he would help her escape.

"No ma'am, I can't do that."

"Oh, yes you can," she insisted. "I have all the money you need outside these walls to pay for your cataract surgery. And if you hope to have that operation, then you help me out of this place."

He reluctantly agreed.

Here was the plan: The next time she heard the toll of the bell, which signaled the death of an inmate, she would slip down to his workroom where he made the caskets. She was to locate the casket in which the old man had placed the corpse and then (if you can imagine!) secretly slide herself into that same casket and pull the top down tightly. Early the next morning the old man would roll her, along with the corpse in the casket, out to the place of burial, drop it into the hole, and dump the dirt on it. The next day he was to come back, uncover the grave, pry the top loose, and set her free. Perfect plan. Almost.

Late one night she heard the deep toll of the bell...someone had died. This was her moment! She secretly slid off her cot, made her way down an eerie hallway, and looking into the dimly lit room she saw the casket. Without hesitation, she lifted the lid and in the darkness slipped into the box and, after squeezing in beside the corpse, she pulled the lid down tightly.

Within a matter of hours she could feel the wheels rolling as they were making their way to the gravesite. She smiled as the casket was placed in the hole. She began to hear the clumps of dirt as they hit the top of the casket. Before long, she was sealed beneath the earth—still smiling.

Silence followed. She could hardly contain her excitement. Time began to drag. The next day came and passed into the night without the old man showing up. By now she has broken into a cold sweat. "Where was he? What could possibly have gone wrong? Why hadn't he shown up?"

In a moment of panic she lights a match and glances at the corpse next to her. You guessed it—*it is the old man himself* who had died!

Slowly, the camera lifts from the gravesite, and all you can hear is the hollow, wailing cry of the woman who will never get out of the grave.

I thought of the proverb, "There is a way that seems right unto a man, but the end thereof are the ways of death." She thought she could escape death's jaws, but the one in whom she had placed her hopes was, himself, a victim of the very thing she dreaded most. She trusted in the wrong man.

One day Jesus Christ will come for us. His coming is sure, and He will keep His promise. Since He has conquered death, He will get us beyond those jaws as well.

If you are ready, the thought of His coming is a comfort. If not, it's a dread. The secret of escape is being sure you know the One who can get us out of the grave. His coming is sure...are you?

1. "Learning in Wartime," *The Weight of Glory and Other Addresses* (New York; Macmillan Company, 1949), 50–51.

THE TROUBLING TRENDS
PORTRAY
HIS COMING

BILLY GRAHAM

Billy Graham, D.D., World-renowned evangelist
Spiritual advisor to six U.S. presidents
Author of bestselling books

We sometimes wonder where God is during the storms of life, in all the troubles of the world. Where is God? Why doesn't He stop the evil? The Bible assures us that God will abolish evil when Christ returns. Someday Christ will come with the shout of acclamation, and there will be a dramatic reunion of all those who have trusted in Him.

No wonder Scripture tells us that at that time "every knee should bow, in heaven and on earth and under the earth, and every tongue confess that Jesus Christ is Lord" (Philippians 2:10–11). If you do not receive Christ as Savior and bow to Him now as Lord of your life, the day is coming when you will bow before Him as Judge.

Jesus did not tell us when He is coming back. He said we were not to speculate. "No one knows about that day or hour, not even the angels in heaven, nor the Son, but only the Father" (Matthew 24:36). The sixth chapter of Revelation gives a strikingly detailed portrait of the end times, but no one knows when these things will be except the Father in Heaven. Not even the angels know. But Jesus also said that there would be certain signs that we could watch for. They are called the "signs of the times," and they are given in detail in chapters 24 and 25 of the Gospel of Matthew—the first book of the New Testament.

Both passages from Matthew and Revelation, taken together, give us a graphic storm warning of events yet to come and provide clearly identifiable signs of the end times. Jesus' own narrative reveals specific details of the fall of Jerusalem and the persecution that would follow. Then in the chapters that follow, Matthew records His triumphal entry into Jerusalem when the crowds hailed Him with palm branches and hosannahs as Messiah. Matthew relates the heartbreaking events of the trials before the Sanhedrin and Pilate, the beatings, the crucifixion, and the thrilling account of Christ's rising from the grave. He provides intimate details of the forty days Jesus spent with the disciples in His glorified body, teaching and challenging them before returning to the throne of Heaven.

But one portion of this story deserves to be examined in greater detail. For when Jesus came up to Jerusalem for that final Passover, He wept over the ancient city. He cried, "O Jerusalem, Jerusalem! The one who kills the prophets and stones those who are sent to her! How often I wanted to gather your children together, as a hen gathers her chicks under her wings, but you were not willing!" (Matthew 23:37 NKJV)

Jesus tried to prepare the disciples for the humiliation He was about to endure—the floggings, the cursings, the mockery, and the shameful death on a cross among thieves—but they did not understand. When He told them He must die and rise again in

three days, they were mystified. Surely He was speaking in parables; no man could die and rise again by his own command—
unless he were God.

As they passed through the city walls, the people with Him
marveled at the size and grandeur of the temple buildings. But
Jesus told them that soon these walls, this temple, and all the
grand palaces and structures in Jerusalem would be flattened, and
"not one stone here will be left on another" (Matthew 24:2).

They were astonished that Jesus would even suggest such a
thing. These were just simple fishermen, tax collectors, and
tradesmen from the remote northern region of Galilee, but they
could see that Jerusalem was a beautiful, grand city. It was the city
hailed by the prophets. How could such towering buildings ever
be flattened? What army, what force, could do such a thing? So a
group of disciples came to Jesus privately and asked Him, "Tell us,
when will these things be? And what will be the sign of Your coming, and of the end of the age?"

THE BEGINNING OF SORROWS

So Jesus sat down with them and began to teach these things. His
answer, recorded in Matthew 24:3–37, offers a dramatic portrait
of the last days of planet Earth. Here Jesus revealed the fate of
Jerusalem, which was carried out to the letter when it was sacked
and burned by the legions of Emperor Titus in A.D. 70. Jesus
spoke of the coming of a godless, secular society, and He spoke of
the dangers of the heresies conceived by false teachers who would
try to pervert the simple message of truth Christ came to deliver.
He said to them: "Take heed that no one deceives you. For many
will come in My name, saying, 'I am the Christ,' and will deceive
many" (Matthew 24:4–5 NKJV).

The rest of the passage, which speaks to the troubles of our own times, reads as follows: "And you will hear of wars and rumors of wars. See that you are not troubled; for all these things must come to pass, but the end is not yet. For nation will rise against nation, and kingdom against kingdom. And there will be famines, pestilences, and earthquakes in various places. All these are the beginning of sorrows."

There has never been a time in history when so many storms have come together in one place and time as they have in the past decade. There have been famines, plagues, and earthquakes for thousands of years, but seldom so many all at once and seldom so concentrated in time and space. The continent of Africa is being devastated by turmoil, famine, and every kind of disease. South America is in political and social chaos. Europe is going through a time of enormous change and uncertainty; only time will reveal the outcome of Eastern Europe as it undergoes the greatest political upheaval in modern times.

In America we see deepening poverty, racial division, homelessness, crime, physical and sexual abuses, and the disintegration of the traditional family. And these storms are further complicated by plagues of many kinds, including AIDS, tuberculosis, and sexually transmitted diseases. Alcoholism, drug addiction, pornography, and other dangerous behaviors are eating away at society. All of these are combined with earthquakes, physical storms, and natural disasters of many kinds all across the land. But Jesus said these are merely a warning of things yet to come. This is merely the beginning of sorrows.

Jesus warned that the price of believing in Him would be high. Mockery, laughter, persecution, even death would be common, but many would refuse to pay such prices. "Then they will deliver you up to tribulation and kill you," He said, "and you will be hated by all nations for My name's sake. And then many will be offended, will betray one another, and will hate one another. Then many false prophets will rise up and deceive many. And because lawlessness will abound, the love of many will grow cold. But he who endures to the end shall be saved."

I believe this is a realistic portrait of our times. Our confidence has been shocked by scandals in the church, in government, in education, and at every level of authority. We have seen graphic images of police officers beating citizens; we have seen top officials of government and business convicted of cheating, lying, and fraud.

We have seen moral and religious leaders, men who claim to be followers of Jesus, fall into disgrace in the eyes of God and man. And worst of all, we have seen the gospel of Jesus Christ twisted and distorted by false teachers to accommodate the destructive morals and secular behavior of these times. These warnings from the Book of Matthew are not parables or myths; they are the very headlines of our day. They are the evidence of Christ's prophecy fulfilled before our eyes.

But the true church would grow through persecution, Jesus said. It would spring forth from darkness and neglect even as the churches of Romania, Bulgaria, and East Germany have sprung full-blown from the soil of despair. "And this gospel of the kingdom will be preached in all the world as a witness to all the nations," He told them, "and then the end will come."

Unfortunately, the desecrations will not end, for a defamer, a desolator, will defile the altar of God and slander Christ and His people. Jesus said, "Therefore when you see the 'abomination of desolation,' spoken of by Daniel the prophet, standing in the holy place (whoever reads, let him understand), then let those within Judea flee to the mountains. Let him who is on the housetop not go down to take anything out of his house. And let him who is in the field not go back to get his clothes. But woe to those who are pregnant and those with nursing babies in those days!"

Just what the nature of that abomination will be is not certain, but it will be a desecration and sacrilege of enormous consequence which will bring about the wrath of God. Then Jesus says,

And pray that your flight may not be in winter or on the Sabbath. For then there will be great tribulation, such as has not been since the beginning of the world until this time, no, nor ever shall be. And unless those days were shortened, no flesh would be saved; but for the elect's sake those days will be shortened. Then if anyone says to you, "Look, here is the Christ!" or "There!" do not believe it. For false christs and false prophets will rise and show great signs and wonders to deceive, if possible, even the elect. See, I have told you beforehand. Therefore if they say to you, "Look, He is in the desert!" do not go out; or "Look, He is in the inner rooms!" do not believe it. For as the lightning comes from the east and flashes to the west, so also will the coming of the Son of Man be. For wherever the carcass is, there the eagles will be gathered together.

THE FINAL HOURS

When the work of the church is nearing fulfillment on earth, Christ told His followers, there would be physical and visible signs that the final days of planet Earth had come. "Immediately after the tribulation of those days," Jesus said, "the sun will be darkened, and the moon will not give its light; the stars will fall from heaven, and the powers of the heavens will be shaken."

The good news for Christians who have remained faithful through trials and persecution will be bad news indeed for everyone who has denied Christ, slandered His people, and followed after false gods.

Jesus told them, "Then the sign of the Son of Man will appear in heaven, and then all the tribes of the earth will mourn, and they will see the Son of Man coming on the clouds of heaven with power and great glory. And He will send His angels with a great sound of a trumpet, and they will gather together His elect from the four winds, from one end of heaven to the other."

Jesus told His followers all of this in concrete and vivid detail. He was not speaking figuratively; this was the unvarnished truth. To be sure that they understood that what he had been telling them was real, not myth or metaphor, He offered the following parable:

Now learn this parable from the fig tree: When its branch has already become tender and puts forth leaves, you know that summer is near. So you also, when you see all these things, know that it is near—at the doors! Assuredly, I say to you, this generation will by no means pass away till all these things take place. Heaven and earth will pass away, but My words will by no means pass away. But of that day and hour no one knows, not even the angels of heaven, but My Father only. But as the days of Noah were, so also will the coming of the Son of Man be.

Matthew 24:32–37 NKJV

By using a story that was clearly a parable, Jesus illustrated that what He had told them about the end of the age was to be considered as a statement of fact. It was not a metaphor, not a myth. In those stunning images we have a glimpse of what the final storm will look like in Christ's own words. This generation—the age of men and women born into the world system by the Greeks and Romans—would survive to see the return of the Messiah. But even as no one had believed Noah's revelation that the flood would come and destroy the world, so in our own time the non-Christian world refuses to believe in the literal return of Jesus Christ. But His return *will* come at a time known only to God.

Imagine how shocking and unsettling these teachings must have been to the disciples of Jesus. Surely they did not fully understand the implications of what He had told them. I suspect that John, the beloved disciple and author of the Apocalypse, came to understand them during his exile on the isle of Patmos, but six decades earlier in A.D. 33 such an understanding would have been utterly inconceivable. Even today many people have difficulty seeing and believing these words.

A TIME TO LIVE

For me, the importance of this stirring passage is not that it gives such vivid detail of the end times, but that it assures us of the eternal security of those who put their trust in Jesus Christ. Suffering and death are nothing to look forward to, but death is not really the issue here; Jesus was talking about the ultimate promise of eternal life with God. That is the truth discovered by the young man who came to our crusade Youth Night in his wheelchair. He could not avoid suffering and death in this life, but He had the thrilling certainty of life with Christ ever after.

All of life resounds with the reality of death. Death is all around us, and it is inevitable in every lifetime. The distinguished British author, C. S. Lewis, once wrote that war does not increase death. As tragic as armed conflict truly is, Lewis pointed out that war does not increase the amount of death in the world, because with or without war, death is universal in every generation. Everybody dies.

The Bible says, "it is appointed unto men once to die" (Hebrews 9:27 KJV). All of nature is in the process of dying, yet most people are living their lives as if they will never die. All over the world men and women are living for today with barely a thought of the possibility of eternity.

Nature teaches that everything which has a beginning has an ending. The day begins with a sunrise, but the sun also sets, the shadows gather, and that calendar day is crossed out, never to come again. We will never be able to repeat today. It is gone forever. The seasons come and go, the decades pass, time moves on, and we grow steadily older. One day each of us will die. That is the promise of the natural world.

Nations rise, they flourish for a time, and then they decline. Eventually every empire comes to an end; not even the greatest can last forever. Time and tide and the ravages of sin take their toll on the most noble achievements of man. This is the decree of history and the way of life on this planet.

The Bible also teaches that the world system as we know it shall come to a close. We read in 1 John 2:17: "And the world is passing away, and the lust of it." Jesus said in Matthew 24:35, "Heaven and earth will pass away…" And in 2 Peter 3:10 we read: "But the day of the Lord will come as a thief in the night, in which the heavens will pass away with a great noise, and the elements will melt with fervent heat; both the earth and the works that are in it will be burned up."

The words of Jesus Christ are good news for a world in crisis. For He gave us a gospel of hope, good news that offers a workable plan for your life, the good news that God loves you, that He is a God of mercy and that He will forgive you if you confess and forsake your sins and have faith in Him.

FAITH IN TIMES OF CRISIS

The marvelous security of the Christian faith is that it is specifically designed for overcoming the storms of this life and giving us the certainty of the life to come in Heaven. The message of Christ proclaims that the world's days are numbered. Every cemetery testifies that this is true. Our days on this planet are numbered. The Scriptures tell us that life is only a vapor that appears for a moment and then vanishes. Our life is like the grass that withers and the flowers that fade. But for those whose hope is in Christ, we know that we shall overcome. The prophet Isaiah, in one of those marvelous passages that foreshadows the coming of Christ, wrote,

> But those who wait on the LORD
> Shall renew their strength;
> They shall mount up with wings like eagles,
> They shall run and not be weary,
> They shall walk and not faint.
>
> Isaiah 40:31 NKJV

That is the hope of every believer.

But there is another sense in which the world system will end; that is, the world itself will end. Someday soon there will be an end of history. That doesn't mean an end to life but the end of a world that has been dominated by greed, evil, and injustice. The fact that the Bible speaks so often and in such graphic detail about the end of the world indicates that God desires that we find security in Him.

The Revelation of John and Christ's teachings in the Book of Matthew tell us that the present world system will pass away and come to a dramatic end. These passages also tell us that Jesus Christ will come again and that He will set up His kingdom of righteousness and social justice where hatred, greed, jealousy, war, and death will no longer exist. Jesus Himself promised the end of the present evil world system and the establishment of a new order, which is called the kingdom of God.

Jesus used images that were dramatic and compelling, but He did not engage in fantasy. He told His followers, "I am the way and the truth, and the life. No one comes to the Father except through Me" (John 14:6), and He was truth and veracity personified. Jesus indicated that when certain things come to pass, we can be assured that the end is near. He said, "You can read the signs of the weather in the sky, but because of spiritual blindness you cannot read the signs of the times." He indicated that only those who have spiritual illumination and discernment from the Holy Spirit can hope to understand the trends and meanings of history.

The Bible plainly indicates that certain conditions will prevail just before the end. For example, the prophet Daniel said, "even to the time of the end…knowledge shall be increased" (Daniel 12:4 KJV). Today there is more knowledge about everything than at any other time in history. I read recently that 90 percent of all the scientists and engineers who have ever lived are alive today. Our high schools, colleges, and universities are turning out millions of graduates every year.

But although our young people are gaining knowledge, they are not always acquiring wisdom to use that knowledge. In every area of life people are floundering, suffering from neuroses and psychological problems on a scale that we have never known before. Our heads are filled with knowledge, but we are confused, bewildered, frustrated, and without moral moorings.

POWER AND GLORY FOREVER

Another condition that the Bible says will be present at the end of the world system is power without peace. Many little wars are taking place all over the world, and certainly a major war could break out at any time. Despite the talk of nuclear disarmament and the end of the Soviet Union, the world is still very much under the threat of nuclear war and nuclear accident.

The United Nations has been battling with Iraq's Saddam Hussein to isolate and destroy his nuclear capabilities, and it is clear that his intentions remain as militant and belligerent as ever. With the proliferation of nuclear arms on every side of the globe, including China, it is not hard to imagine that somebody could push the wrong button or miscalculate. In a matter of seconds the world could be plunged into a third world war that nobody wants. Jesus said, "And you will hear of wars and rumors of wars... For nation will rise against nation, and kingdom against kingdom" (Matthew 24:6–7 NKJV).

But as the United Nations attempts to mediate hostilities in dozens of nations around the globe, the world is still an armed camp. Billions of dollars, rubles, marks, and pounds are spent for weapons that quickly become obsolete or are replaced with newer ones which cost even more. The United States alone spends hun-

dreds of billions of dollars on armaments. In short, the atmosphere of the world is still threatening. While the world cries,
"Peace, peace," there is no peace.

I often hear people ask, "Why is there so little peace in the
world when we have such unprecedented knowledge and unlim-
ited potential?" We are trying to build a peaceful world, but there
is no peace within people's hearts. The Los Angeles riots were, as
every reporter noted, evidence of a deep-seated anger and bitter-
ness welling up in America's soul. The Bible assures us that we
cannot build a new world on the old, unregenerate hearts of people. The new world will only come about when Jesus Christ, King
of kings and Lord of lords, reigns supreme.

Most of us are familiar with these memorable words from
Handel's famous oratorio, *The Messiah,* taken from the writings of
the prophet Isaiah:

> For unto us a Child is born,
> Unto us a Son is given;
> And the government will be upon His shoulder.
> And His name will be called
> Wonderful, Counselor, Mighty God,
> Everlasting Father, Prince of Peace.
> Of the increase of His government and peace
> There will be no end,
> Upon the throne of David and over His kingdom,
> To order it and establish it with judgment and justice
> From that time forward, even forever.
> The zeal of the LORD of hosts will perform this.
>
> Isaiah 9:6–7 NKJV

These words are the best promise of security in a world of tension and turmoil. The Kings of kings is the hope of every man, woman, and child of every tribe and nation that knows the name of Christ. His kingdom is forever.

The signs of insecurity and the shouts of revolution heard around the world are perhaps the death rattle of an era in civilization—perhaps they signal the end of civilization as we have known it. In either event, it is now God's turn to act, and Scripture promises that He will act dramatically. He will send His Son, Jesus Christ, back to this earth. He is the Lord of history. The storms of change in the former Soviet Union are no surprise to Him; nothing we have seen in the headlines is taking God by surprise. Events are moving rapidly toward some sort of climax, but it will be according to God's timing, when His Son returns to be the rightful ruler of the world.

Before that time comes, however, God wants to rule in our hearts. He sent His Son into the world to be the ruler of our hearts. The Bible says that sin shall not have dominion over us if Jesus Christ is in our hearts as Lord and Master. The danger lies in the fact that there are two rulers who want to control us: our self and Jesus Christ. Either self will reign in our lives, or Jesus Christ will reign. "No one can serve two masters," Jesus said (Matthew 6:24). The Bible challenges us, "choose for yourselves this day whom you will serve" (Joshua 24:15 NKJV).

Solomon wrote in the Proverbs, "There is a way that seems right to a man, but in the end it leads to death" (Proverbs 14:12). If you want to have peace with God and find security for these times of trouble, you must answer one very important question: *Who is the ruler of your life?* Are you trying to be the master of your own fate? Are you trying to be the captain of your own soul? Do you believe you can navigate life's storms without the Master at the helm? Or is the kingdom of God within you?

Jesus Christ can come into your heart right now if you will turn from your sins and receive Him as Savior. He loves you. He knows you by name, and He wants to forgive you. You can enter the new kingdom, the new world that will be born under His leadership when He comes again. There is no doubt that the world to come will be a theocracy, but it will be a joyous, exciting, incredibly beautiful place with Jesus Christ in complete and loving control.

THE PROPHETS
PROMISED
HIS COMING

STANLEY ELLISEN

Stanley Ellisen, Th.D.
Professor of Biblical literature emeritus
Western Conservative Baptist Seminary
Author of numerous books.

Most human predictions are about as reliable as Felix the cat. They change with the seasons. We can't see around the corner, let alone into the future. Predicting the sunrise, of course, isn't too difficult, and even the whims of the weather we can occasionally anticipate. Where human nature is involved, however, prognostication is the sport of clairvoyants or gamblers. Computers are of little help here—too naive with the facts, too unimaginative. The particular whim people will follow is anybody's guess, Pavlov's dog notwithstanding.

God, however, is above the clairvoyants, forecasters, and even Pavlov's dog. His foresight is as sharp as His hindsight; He is Lord of the future. Individuals may dabble in general prognoses of guess and hope, but God specializes in specific details of the future. As we have noted, He has claimed a monopoly in the field. To demonstrate this aspect of His sovereignty, the Lord endowed certain men with the ability to "sightsee" the future. These men were called prophets in the Old Testament, and forecasting the future became their badge of authenticity (Isaiah 41:21–23; Daniel 2:28).

THE WORK OF THE PROPHETS

The prophets of Israel go back to the founding fathers, Abraham, Moses, and Samuel (Genesis 20:7; Deuteronomy 18:15; 1 Samuel 3:20). Unlike the offices of priest and king, however, they were not restricted to specific families or tribes. Several prophetesses were also raised up for this emergency service, commanding the attention of the nation. These prophets of Israel can be listed in two general groups, the "speaking prophets" (18) and the "writing prophets" (16). Most of the "writing prophets" came on the scene after the "speaking prophets," recording specific messages from the Lord.

The times of the writing prophets of Israel were mainly in the latter stages of Israel's history. They were raised up as special heralds in times of great national crises. Most of them came on the scene when idolatry and degeneration were rampant and judgment was about to fall. Their tenure was often when the kings and priests had departed from God's Law and the covenant of blessing. Thus they spoke to the people long after the covenants had been established. Their mission was to call the nation to repentance and righteousness that the covenant promises might be fulfilled. In the process they were used of God to fill in many of the details of that prophetic program. What the covenants had outlined, in other words, the writing prophets detailed in many specific ways.

These prophets of Israel came to be practically an institution in themselves. A rugged and stern breed of individuals, they were called of God to fulfill an assignment of alerting the nation that was anything but popular. Coming from outside the system, they spoke with thundering power to the whole society of kings, priests, and people. In a sense, they constituted the nagging conscience of the nation. Preachers they were, but not mere finger-pointers or ritualists. Their appearance was often a solemn omen: God was about to speak in judgment or deliverance. Though frequently reviled as they spoke, they were later exonerated and revered as their judgments came to pass. They left the people no doubt that a mighty prophet had been among them.

It was through these doughty saints that God chose to unveil many details of His future program. As the covenants provided the skeleton of that program, the prophets boldly described details of its life and substance.

The content of the prophets' messages touched many aspects of life, but we can summarize them under the two concepts of judgment and blessing. They warned of judgment for sin and promised blessing for repentance and obedience. Many of their words were historically fulfilled, but many others concerned things to come. They both addressed the needs of their own generations and envisioned what God would do in the distant future. Their prophetic binoculars, in other words, often had both close-range and telescopic lenses.

Our concern, however, is with the end-time program when God will culminate His purposes in the earth. By looking through their telescopic lenses we can get a broad perspective of the prophetic end-times by highlighting their emphasis on judgment and blessing. These can be seen by reviewing two of their central themes: "The judgments of the coming day of the Lord," and "The blessing of the coming of Messiah."

THE JUDGMENTS OF THE COMING DAY
OF THE LORD

This first prophetic theme of "judgment" in the day of the Lord, brings up a concept that is anything but popular today. To many it is downright contemptible, a leaf out of savagery, and incompatible with Christian love. Religion, we are told, should be attractive, soothing, and appealing. If God is both loving and almighty, why all this talk about judgment?

The popular view of God as an indulgent grandfather may be folksy and "Good Ol' Charlie Brown" theology, but it is not found in the Bible. Though the Bible does have much to say of God's love in Christ, it also reveals His anger and coming wrath on sin. It has more to say about judgment, in fact, than about any other subject (as seen in the Old Testament prophets and the words of Jesus).

Several kinds of judgment are described, but the one most frequently spoken of in the Old Testament is that of the day of the Lord. Franz Delitzsch, the great Old Testament scholar of Germany, called this term the "watchword of prophecy." It is used twenty times in the Hebrew Bible and adverted to countless other times (some 75 as "that day"). Though it concludes with the great age of Messianic blessings, the prophets especially emphasized this coming day of judgment or world accounting. Since the judgments of that day loom so large in their view of the future, it is essential that we grasp their overall meaning as they related it to future events.

The Day of the Lord Identified

The day of the Lord in its simplest form means "God's day," in contrast to "man's day." It can be thought of as a special time when God steps into human affairs to assume direct control, whether in judgment or blessing. It does not necessarily mean a single day of twenty-four hours, but rather a specific time period. Such, for instance, was the time of the great flood of Genesis which lasted over a year; the judgment of the locust plague in Joel 1; and the destruction of Jerusalem by Nebuchadnezzar who is said to have wielded the "sword of the Lord" (Zephaniah 1).

More specifically, however, it is the day when He will grab the reins of world affairs to fulfill His covenant promises of judgment and blessing. In this more technical sense the prophets spoke of it as a specific time in the future when God will bring the nations of the world to account. This divine accounting seems to relate especially to the Noahic covenant, as we shall presently note.

The time limits of that future period can be seen more precisely from its use in the New Testament. In 2 Thessalonians 2:3, Paul declares that the day of the Lord will begin when the antichrist appears. His appearance will mark the commencement of that period when God will use this wicked king to polarize all antigod forces shortly before their destruction. Its end will come after the millennial age and God's renewal of heaven and earth, as Peter notes in his final epistle (2 Peter 3:10). These references indicate that the entire period of the day of the Lord will extend over a thousand years from the beginning of the tribulation period to the final purging of the earth for the eternal state.

The preponderant usage of this term, however, concerns that time of world judgment just prior to Christ's return, known as the "tribulation period." This is evidently the same period referred to by Daniel as the "seventieth week" of Israel. It is basically that end-time period, often described in the Bible, when God will bring judgment and wrath on the nations as they unite in rebellion against Him. That time of judgment, however, will relate to both Israel and the world at large.

Judgement on the World

The Prophets practically made a saw of the principle that judgment must precede blessing. Before the earth can experience the reign of Messiah, it must be purged of its sin and lawlessness. David in his second Psalm portrayed this coming judgment as a time of God's wrath poured out on a raging world, whose leaders have formed a conspiracy against God's "Anointed" (Psalm 2). Joel, one of the first writing prophets, also described it as a day of darkness unparalleled in human history (Joel 2:1–2). He described it as a time of destruction from the Almighty, the "fireworks" of which would reach to the starry heavens (Joel 1:15; 2:30f.).

This world judgment is many times emphasized by Isaiah, the evangelical prophet of the late eighth century. In his "Little Apocalypse" of chapter 24, for instance, he envisioned the earth as being utterly spoiled as a result of man's transgression of God's laws.

That desolation will be so great that few inhabitants of the earth will survive (24:6). He saw the earth as reeling to and fro and the sun and moon as being ashamed. The specific reason for this divine judgment Isaiah attributed to the nations' failure to keep the everlasting covenant (Isaiah 24:5). This is obviously the Noahic covenant, the only everlasting covenant given to the nations as such (Genesis 9:5–11). The implication is that God will judge the nations for their failure to restrain evil and maintain moral righteousness.

This intense period of God's wrath on the nations is also spoken of by Daniel the prophet in exile. He described it as a "time of distress such as never occurred since there was a nation until that time" (Daniel 12:1). His prophecy especially emphasized the part Antichrist will play in the final drama. He saw this dark fig-

ure as the human agent especially responsible for igniting the
international horror. Following a meteoric rise to power after
which he coerces the world to satanic idolatry, this fierce, godless,
world dictator will assemble the nations of the world against Jerusalem in vengeance against God. Except for the supernatural help
of Michael the archangel, even the elect of God would be
destroyed in this holocaust (Daniel 12:1; cf. Matthew 24:21–22).

The climactic event of the period, as the prophets portray it,
will be the coming of Messiah Himself. Isaiah 63 describes His
coming in the role of a "man of war," treading down His enemies
in anger and fury. His coming will make the earth to tremble
(2:21). Of this the New Testament has much to say in the consummation book of Revelation. Although the Lord will personally
orchestrate this entire judgment on the nations from heaven, He
will finally descend Himself to the place of judgment to complete
the job—to "thoroughly purge his floor."

These Old Testament passages stress the fact that God has set
a day in which He will judge the nations. He will call them to
account for perpetuating wickedness in the earth. Though He is
longsuffering, He has not forgotten the wickedness of the unre-
pentant. He has not watered down His standards of righteousness
or declared some kind of universal amnesty as a compromise with
man's penchant to sin. His hatred for sin has not assuaged. The
day of the Lord will demonstrate His wrath against those who
despise both His law and His grace.

Judgment on the Nation Israel

This warning of coming wrath on the nations should have struck
fear and awe in the most calloused hearts of Israel. The irony is
that the opposite took place. They rejoiced at this condemnation

of the heathen. The self-righteous of the nation saw it as their day of vengeance on their adversaries. To them it was just recompense for their voracious onslaughts against them. This attitude is especially reflected in the book of Jonah where even the prophet hoped for their destruction rather than their salvation.

Many of the prophets, however, condemned this attitude and warned the nation of it (that was the point of Jonah's message). In staccato words of warning they sought to arouse the nation: "Alas, you who are longing for the day of the Lord," said Amos. "For what purpose will the day of the Lord be to you? It will be darkness and not light" (Amos 5:18). Far from being exempt from that judgment, they declared that Israel will actually be the vortex or focal point of much of that terror. Most of the prophets speak of this final purging of the nation.

The Bible references to this period of intense trial for Israel date back to Moses and the covenants. As he spoke his final words to Israel, he lamented that in the distant future they would be scattered among the nations. The covenants did not immune them from judgment. The later prophets also emphasized this theme as they came to warn both kingdoms in their times of national apostasy. Joel in the south, for instance, decried the drunkenness and dead ritualism of Judah and Jerusalem, pleading for repentance. Amos in the north, eloquently pleaded for their return to righteousness, condemning their blatant carnality as the nation plunged toward destruction. As they basked in the prosperity and pleasure of the golden age of Jeroboam II, this shepherd-prophet scored them with his bony finger of condemnation. Though he included the heathen in his roster of judgment, he saved his most explosive salvos for Israel. The nation, he declared, would bear the brunt of that judgment, for she had more than her share of sinners, most of whom knew better, but willfully disdained that knowledge.

As Amos spoke to the North prior to its captivity, so Jeremiah spoke to the South as it also careened to destruction in the following century (625–586). His prophecy, however, envisioned also a distant judgment for both nations. While announcing immediate judgment at the hands of Babylon, he foresaw also a day of travail in the distant future for both Israel and Judah. "Alas! for that day is great, so that none is like it: it is even the time of Jacob's trouble" (Jeremiah 30:3–7). Following this time of final tribulation, however, the prophet declared that a remnant would be saved, after which both nations would be regathered in peace and spiritual unification. This prophecy spoken while Judah was on the skids, obviously refers to the time of Israel's final regathering at Christ's return. Then "—David their king, whom I will raise up for them," will reign over the whole nation as he serves under Christ the King of kings (Jeremiah 30:9).

The Great and Terrible Day of the Lord

Several prophets refer to the day of the Lord as the "great and terrible [dreadful] day of the Lord" (Joel 2:31; Zephaniah 1:14; Malachi 4:5). They suggest that part of that period will be of special intensity, a fact also noted by the New Testament. Interestingly, these three prophets spoke at the beginning, middle, and end of the prophetic era, about two hundred years apart (830; 630; 430). Joel, one of the first writing prophets, noted that this intense wrath would begin with certain heavenly signs and disturbances. The sun will "be turned into darkness and the moon into blood" before the great and terrible day of the Lord (Joel 2:31). This is similar to Zephaniah's description (1:14f) and almost identical to that of the Apostle John in Revelation 6:12–17.

Malachi also reminded the nation of this divine day of judg-ment in his final message of the Old Testament. His last words alerted them to a special sign the Lord would send to commence that day (Malachi 4:5–6). That sign will be the return of Elijah the prophet for a special ministry to the nation. As with other judg-ments, God's wrath is often preceded by warnings. Malachi saw the Lord's "striking the earth with a curse" as contingent on their response to Elijah's coming and powerful ministry. This appears to be what John also refers to in Revelation 11, as he describes the two witnesses in the end-times. Their "power to shut heaven so that no rain falls in the days of their prophecy" (3 1/2 yrs.), almost certainly alludes to this return of Elijah who began his judgment ministry in the time of idolatrous Ahab by calling for a drought (1 Kings 17:1).

This time of great and terrible distress for Israel Jesus called the "great tribulation" (Matthew 24:21). It will be a brief period of unprecedented trial followed by His own return in glory. Though the people of Israel have known unrelieved suffering through much of their history, Jesus said their greatest crucible lies ahead. For rea-sons not entirely of their own making, they have certainly not yet recognized Jesus as their Messiah. Doubtless the Church bears part of the blame for alienating them, but there is yet little sign of a turn-around. However, at the conclusion of this final purge, the whole nation will mourn for Him as they see His wounded hands and side (Zechariah 12). Though traumatic for all involved, it will accom-plish its divine purpose of salvaging a purified remnant for the new society of Israel in the Messianic kingdom.

These passages reveal the great concern of the prophets for the coming day of the Lord. They saw it as a future period in world history when the sovereign Lord will call the world to account. He will judge them for their non-response to His sovereignty as Lord of the nations. This judgment will serve several salutary purposes in the divine plan. It will first demonstrate the natural consequences of sin in a world raging with passions and independence of God. In that short period it will show what a horrible holocaust sin can bring on a world when briefly allowed to go unrestrained.

Secondly, it will give an ominous demonstration of God's solemn view of lawlessness and rebellion. It will show that His patience with sin in the world does have an end. The Bible's portrayal of God's wrath against sin will be seen to be more than just a pious myth of divine fuming. It will confirm that His longsuffering, though long, is not endless.

Finally, the judgment of that day will cleanse the earth to prepare it for Messiah's kingdom of righteousness. As the world of Noah's time was scrubbed by water, so the earth will again be cleansed for a new beginning of peace and righteousness. That will usher in the blessing era of the day of the Lord. As the Hebrew day began with a period of darkness followed by a period of sunshine, so the darkness of the day of the Lord will be followed by the sunshine of Messiah's coming. He will come as "The Sun of Righteousness…with healing in His wings" (Malachi 4:2).

THE BLESSINGS OF MESSIAH'S COMING

The second grand theme of the prophets is that of the coming of Messiah, often called "the Servant of the Lord." His Person and coming, of course, are central to the whole of Scripture, but are especially prominent in the prophets. Though they often begin their prophecies with warnings of the day of the Lord, they almost invariably conclude by alluding to the coming of Messiah and His kingdom. His coming is the stream of hope and joy in their messages. To get a taste of this content, let's recall the meaning of the name "Messiah," and then look at the person and work of Messiah as described by the prophets.

Messiah means the "Anointed One" (translated "Christ" in the New Testament). In Old Testament times, Israel's leaders were usually anointed for service. This gave them distinction among the people and divine power to execute their work. Their being anointed with oil spoke of the Spirit's presence and power working in them. Whether as prophet, priest, or king, they were acknowledged as the Lord's servant-leaders by this anointing.

There was, however, a unique Person that the prophets looked for who was to be the supreme Servant of the Lord, anointed as Messiah. Though only Daniel used this title (9:25–26), the other descriptions of Him assume this special anointing. His coming was the central hope of the Old Testament, for it was He who would deliver His people. Since so many myths and legends later grew up around this messianic concept, it is important to identify Him from the Prophets themselves.

His Role as Servant of the Lord

The prophet Isaiah is often called the Messianic prophet, though the Psalms and Zechariah also have this emphasis. Prominent in Isaiah is the designation, "Servant of the Lord." This title suggests that this coming One would be both human and divine, the Son of David and the Son of God. Isaiah 9:6 describes Him as both a child born and Almighty God. His name, in fact, would be Immanuel, "God with us."

This twofold portrayal of Messiah is also drawn by Zechariah who described Him as being pierced as a man and as the Lord

(YHWH) Himself (12:10; 14:34). The blending of these two natures by the prophets is quite common in the Psalms, and is, of course, explained and expanded in the New Testament. John the Apostle, for instance, referred to this hypostatic union of God and man in Messiah by showing Him as both the eternal Creator and yet made flesh to dwell among us (John 1; Isaiah 40:28).

This title, Servant of the Lord, then suggests His coming to do God's service. As such, He would accomplish God's work, fulfilling His kingdom and redemptive purposes in the earth. This work of Messiah may be reviewed by recalling the three offices He was to fulfill: prophet, priest, and king. As a fulfillment of these sacred offices, Messiah was to be the final Prophet, Priest, and King. He would far outrank Moses the first prophet, Melchizedek the first priest, and David the first king.

To appreciate His Servant work, it will help to review these Old Testament offices and how they served as types of this great antitype. They portray Messiah as the final Revealer, final Redeemer, and final Ruler for God in the earth.

His Role as Prophet

The prophetic work of Messiah was first introduced by Moses the first prophet (Deuteronomy 18:15). This he did as he was preparing to leave Israel under Joshua's leadership. Stressing the importance of giving heed to God's word through the appointed leaders, he also announced that another Prophet would one day arise, to whom they had better give earnest heed.

For what purpose, we might ask, was Messiah to come as a prophet? The special work of prophets was to speak for God. They were His special ombudsmen, whether as forth-tellers or foretellers. Often their messages were accompanied by miraculous credentials, especially in the presence of strong resistance. Moses, for instance, performed many miracles in Egypt where he had to convince the people that he spoke from God. Likewise, Elijah and Elisha wrought mighty miracles as they denounced the idolatry of Baal in Israel. Miracles were signs from heaven to command attention and underscore their divine authority as they confronted unbelief.

Those miracles of the prophets were a kind of foretaste of what the Prophet Messiah would do. His miracles, however, would be far more numerous. They would, in fact, constitute His credentials as the final Prophet from God. Like the prophets of old, He would do His mighty works in the power of the Holy Spirit (Isaiah 11:2; 42:1; 61:1). In this power He would heal the sick and judge the wicked in the presence of great opposition (Isaiah 35:4–6; 42:1–4).

The preeminent work of the Old Testament prophets, however, was not performing miracles, but proclaiming God's message. Moses was famous for his miraculous works, but he was far more distinguished for his mighty words. He was especially known as the lawgiver. Likewise, this final Prophet, whom he introduced, was to be preeminently known for his mighty words (Deuteronomy 18:18). He would, in fact, be the outstanding revelation of God, far superseding Moses as the voice and Word of God. John in the New Testament constantly identifies Jesus in this way. As the living Word, He came to reveal both the character of the Father and His final message to men (Hebrews 1:1–2).

The Old Testament, then, saw the coming of Messiah as God's Prophet par excellence. His prophetic ministry would be backed up with the staccato power of miracles, arousing all to the fact that God had again spoken to His people, this time by One far greater than Moses (Hebrews 1:2). This prophetic work was the first important aspect of Messiah's ministry as the Servant of the Lord.

His Role as Priest

Israel, however, needed more than a prophet; she needed a priest. Besides revelation, she needed redemption. Though in covenant relation with the Lord, her most basic need was atonement for sin. To fill this need for Israel and all mankind, Messiah would come not only as a prophet but also as a priest. He would, in fact, be the ultimate and final High Priest. David made this point in Psalm 110:4: "The Lord has sworn and will not relent, 'You are a priest forever according to the order of Melchizedek.'" Later writers also elaborated on this high priestly work of Messiah.

His priestly functions. To appreciate the significance of Messiah's priestly work, we need to recall the primary functions of the Old Testament priests. Their work involved two basic functions: making atonement for sin and making intercession for sinners. At the brazen altar of the temple they offered sacrifices for sin; on the basis of that offering they then offered incense in the holy place and made intercession for sinners. The prophet Isaiah nicely summarized this work as he applied it to the coming Messiah: "He bore the sins of many, and made intercession for the transgressors" (Isaiah 53:12). In contrast to the work of a prophet who spoke to men for God, the priest spoke to God for men. He was God's ordained channel of approach to Himself on the basis of the atoning blood (Leviticus 17:11). The priest was the divinely appointed mediator between God and man.

His qualifications. To perform this work the priest had to have special qualifications. Not just anyone could assume the office. The New Testament book of Hebrews summarizes the Levitical code by noting two basic requirements for a priest (Hebrews 5:1–4). First, he had to be "taken from among men"—that is, a genuine representative of man. As man's attorney before God, he had to understand the human dilemma by walking in the sandals of men.

Second, he had to be ordained by God—that is, he could not just take up the vocation on his own. A special anointing or approval by God was required for him to stand before the Almighty. Likewise, Jesus "became to all those who obey him the sources of eternal salvation" (Hebrews 5:9). These two basic qualifications of a priest in the Old Testament were supremely fulfilled in Christ.

Isaiah 53 gives a classic portrayal of the Servant of the Lord fulfilling these high priestly functions. This passage is really the high point of the Old Testament in describing Messiah's atoning work. Isaiah, the "prince of prophets," constructs a beautiful symmetry around this imperial chapter, as well as within it. The twenty-seven chapters of the second half of the book (40–66) are divided into three sections of nine chapters each, with a similar conclusion in each, "There is no peace for the wicked" (the last chapter describing it). Also the central chapter of each section highlights the theme of that section and they all converge around chapter 53. This symmetry may be seen in a pyramidal outline that builds up to and flows from the majestic peak of this central chapter.

I. THE GREATNESS OF GOD AS SOVEREIGN CREATOR, ISAIAH 40–48
    40. His greatness as a sovereign Shepherd
    41. His greatness to deliver Israel
    42. His greatness as a "Servant"
    43. His greatness to save the undeserving
    44. His greatness contrasted with idols

45. His greatness to unshackle through Cyrus

46. His greatness over Babylon's idols

47. His greatness to judge proud Babylon

48. His greatness to purge obstinate Israel

II. THE GRACE OF GOD AS SUFFERING SAVIOR, ISAIAH
49–57

49. The Lord's Servant as a world-wide Savior

50. The Lord's Servant deplores Israel's divorce

51. The Lord's Servant to save in righteousness

52. The Lord's Servant prepares to bring salvation

AS "LAMB"

53. The Lord's Servant offers Himself as atonement for sin

54. His salvation extended to Israel in remarriage

55. His salvation extended to all the world

56. His salvation extended to the responsive

57. His salvation extended to the worst of sinners

III. THE GLORY OF GOD AS ROYAL RESTORER, ISAIAH
58–66

58. Israel's religious depravity deplored

59. Israel's social depravity declared

60. Israel's future righteousness and glory

61. Israel's Bridegroom coming with jewels

62. Israel's royal remarriage in righteousness

63. Israel's great revenge at the Lord's return

64. Israel's remnant in deep penitence

65. Israel's purging for millennial glory

66. Israel's rebirth in humility and joy

This symmetry is further seen in that the central chapter of each section (44; 53; 62) epitomizes the emphasis of that section, and all the chapters converge on the "unbelievable report" of 53. Also the central four verses of 53 (5–8) constitute the heart of the gospel: after being rejected and pierced by men, the Suffering Servant bore our sins as "the Lord laid on Him the iniquities of us all." And amazingly, the central word of this central chapter in the Greek Septuagint text (144th of 290) is the identification of this Servant as the "lamb" (53:7). Messiah's work as the Lamb of God is central to Isaiah's theme, as it is also to the whole Bible.

Isaiah concludes this chapter on the Suffering Servant with a succinct summary of the work of a priest. Though rejected and numbered with transgressors, the prophet says of this One that He "bore the sins of many and made intercession for the transgressors." That, of course, was the twofold work of the Old Testament priest who beautifully typified the high priestly work of Messiah.

An Old Testament mystery resolved. Though His priesthood is amply stated in the Old Testament, it is not left without problems. Unresolved is the mystery of how He could be a priest if He came from the wrong tribe—the tribe of Judah, rather than the priestly tribe of Levi. This problem is not answered, in fact, until the New Testament book of Hebrews where the writer addresses this lingering dilemma. There he makes the point three times that Christ's priesthood was not of the Levitical order of Aaron, but of the superior order of Melchizedek (Hebrews 5:6–10; 6:20; 7:1–17). It was superior in that even Abraham paid homage to Melchizedek. Like Melchizedek, this Priest would be one of a kind, without predecessor or successor. He would be the final and ultimate Priest before God. This is so important to the Hebrews writer that he turns the whole argument of his book on this point. The obsolescence of the old covenant with its ritual system rested on this accession of Christ as the final Priest for both Israel and the Church (Hebrews 7:12). Only in Christ could this Old Testament mystery of Messiah's priesthood be resolved.

His Role as King

The most heralded function of Messiah, as prophesied in the Old Testament, was doubtless His coming as king. He was to be King of Israel and of the world. Not only would He reveal truth as Prophet and redeem men as Priest, but would also rule the earth as King. This reigning role of a glorious king, of course, became the beatific vision of the nation. It buoyed their spirits with hope, especially in later times as they grovelled under the heel of Gentile oppressors.

Promised in the covenants. The basis of this vision of Messiah as King derives originally from Jacob's blessing on his son Judah (Genesis 49). That blessing, however, was based on the Abrahamic covenant (2 Samuel 7:12–16; Psalm 2:6), which was further elaborated in the Davidic covenant. To David the Lord promised a son that would reign over Israel forever. Isaiah also referred to this when he spoke of Messiah's coming from the royal house of David (Isaiah 11:1). David evidently cogitated much over this promise, for his Psalms make frequent mention of such a coming King (e.g., Psalm 2:2, 6–12; 24:7–10; 89:3–4, 34–37; 110:1, 5–6).

Portrayed by the prophets. The most explicit portrayal of this coming King, however, is given by the prophet Zechariah. His vivid description is progressively developed throughout his book. In his final chapter he shows how He will come in judgment following a massive confrontation of nations against Jerusalem. This picture is not pretty, detailing a great slaughter of Israel and the nations, climaxed by the descent of Messiah to avenge His people. As He comes He trounces all His enemies, making the earth to tremble with earthquakes and nuclear disasters. The prophet's final portrayal depicts Messiah as "King over all the earth," receiving homage from all nations who come to Jerusalem to worship (Zechariah 14:9, 16).

Zechariah's description of Messiah's coming, however, appears to be somewhat paradoxical, if not contradictory. Before picturing Him coming as a mighty King, he sketches Him coming in meekness and humility. Rather than riding a monarch's white steed, He comes riding a lowly burro (Zechariah 9:9). To complicate it further, he later portrays Him as One who has been pierced in the house of His friends (Zechariah 12:10; 13:6). This Shepherd of Israel, he declared, would be smitten and the sheep scattered. What kind of Messiah is this?

This anomaly is difficult to harmonize apart from the New Testament. Its unexplained tension is seen in many of the prophets, but never entirely relieved. Nor could it have been by the very nature of events that would bring it about. Jewish commentaries even today are nonplussed by it, many regarding the book of Zechariah an insoluble enigma. Some have sought to explain it by the idea that two different messiahs were promised in the Old Testament, a suffering servant and a conquering prince. One they identify as "son of Joseph," and the other as "son of David" (Edersheim, *Jesus the Messiah*, II 434–35). This notion, however, is not derived from the Old Testament, but was a later concoction of the second century A.D. They used it to explain the Roman slaying of Bar Kokhba who claimed to be Messiah.

This problem, of course, dissolves in the New Testament after the actual crucifixion of Christ. He Himself explained that His second coming in glory would be entirely different from His first coming in humility. Though He came the first time as the Suffering Servant to atone for sin, He will come the second time as the conquering King to judge and rule the world.

In retrospect we recall that David had a similar experience in becoming king, in many ways typifying Christ. Before he gained his throne, he suffered many injustices from jealous King Saul and went through a long period of exile. He gave a living portrayal of Messiah, his greater Son. The promised Messiah would experience both of these roles in infinite degree to fulfill His mission of both Redeemer and ruling Sovereign over the earth.

His Kingdom

In describing a king and his work it would be unthinkable not to refer also to his kingdom. Likewise, the Old Testament has much to say of the messianic kingdom. King Messiah will not be an abstract King, but will reign over a kingdom. As we previously noted, that rule will involve not only His authority, but a territory and people over which He reigns. Most of the Prophets speak of this Old Testament portrayal of His kingdom, but especially those of Isaiah and Ezekiel.

Isaiah's vision of the kingdom. The prophecy of Isaiah is most unique in its emphasis on salvation, but he also had much to say of the coming kingdom of Messiah. His predictions cover many aspects of Israel's life, both historic and prophetic. Concerning that coming kingdom, he spoke of its spiritual, social, political, and physical features. Though he thoroughly rebuked their increasing depravity, he also envisioned a bright future beyond their final purging with many changes occurring in their national life.

A sampling of these might be noted: a small righteous remnant will be preserved and regathered from all parts of the world. The land itself will be rejuvenated to blossom and fill the earth with fruit. Righteousness will cover the earth; health and productivity will flourish; and even the animal kingdom will be at peace (Isaiah 11; 25; 27; 35; 65). He notes also that Israel under Messiah will be the superpower among the nations, Jerusalem will be the world capital, and universal peace will cover the earth. All this the prophet envisioned as coming to pass by virtue of Messiah's redemptive work and His personal presence among His people.

This glowing picture of a reunited nation is painted by this first Major Prophet, but he frankly discerns it as a distant hope for the faithful, beyond their present morass of sin and depravity.

Jeremiah's vision. Jeremiah followed Isaiah nearly one hundred years later but gave comparatively little space to the future kingdom. This weeping prophet was so overwhelmed by Judah's mounting rebellion, he spent most of his time warning of impending disaster. In the midst of that, however, he did provide a glimmer of light in the distant future concerning their broken covenant. As previously noted, chapters 30–33 speak of Israel's final restoration as guaranteed by the Abrahamic and Davidic covenants. Having declared in chapter 11 that they would experience God's curse for having broken the Mosaic covenant, he here announced that the Lord will one day institute a new covenant to replace the old. This new agreement will embrace both kingdoms when they are regathered in the land and regenerated. Jeremiah was careful to emphasize that these spiritual blessings would come after their final period of tribulation which he called "Jacob's trouble" (Jeremiah 30:7).

Ezekiel's vision. This third Major Prophet was also a priest, but he ministered to the captive Jews in faraway Babylon. As a godly cleric, he gave the priestly version of their captivity in Babylon, showing its cause to be their sins of idolatry and temple defilement. For this he saw the Lord write "Ichabod" over the land, portraying the "Glory" making a reluctant departure from the temple (Ezekiel 11:22 f.).

In his final chapters (40–48), however, he pictured the return of that Glory in the distant future along with the restoration of Israel's worship system. Not only will Jerusalem be rebuilt, but the temple also will be reconstructed with entirely new dimensions. Though similar to previous sanctuaries, that future temple will have some striking differences. Absent will be the ark of the covenant, the lampstand, the table of show bread, the mercy seat, the cherubim, the altar of incense, and the vail. A most amazing omission is the absence of a high priest, though other priests are mentioned.

These apparent errors are not explained and seem unconscionable for this priest turned architect—unless he had a special reason for leaving them out. On further reflection, however, that reason becomes obvious. The fact that Messiah Himself will be there in Person is reason enough. He will be there as the true essence of the Law, the Lampstand, the Show Bread, the Mercy Seat, etc. In that future kingdom, He will not only be the King on the throne, but also the recognized High Priest of Israel. His personal presence there explains those missing parts and serves also to confirm the actual rebuilding of that future temple. It is consistent, as well, with Ezekiel's earlier prophecies, all of which were fulfilled historically in a quite literal way, almost with a vengeance.

Summary of the Prophets

As the covenants were given to outline and guarantee God's program, the prophets later came to fill in the details. They came as God's special envoys in times of spiritual declension, calling the people back from disaster. As they rebuked the nation for sin, they also alerted them to the grandeurs of a fantastic future promised God's people.

Central to all their prophecies was the coming of the divine Servant of the Lord, later called Messiah. This One would minister to the nation as the true Prophet, Priest, and King. His coming, however, always presented a bit of a mystery, for He was to come as both a Suffering Servant and a conquering King. Though these roles were not clearly sorted out, the prophets described His mission as bringing both spiritual deliverance from sin and national deliverance from their enemies.

From Abraham to John the Baptist His coming was longingly anticipated, especially in times of exile and foreign oppression. That glorious coming, however, came to tantalize different people in different ways, depending on their spiritual outlook. Some looked for spiritual redemption and a deliverer from sin; others were more concerned for national deliverance and economic welfare. That they could have the second without the first, however, was nowhere suggested by the prophets. The spiritual had to precede the material and political.

The further questions of when and how these events were to occur, however, remained enigmas to most of the prophets. Not that these were foolish and impious questions, but they were just not discussed. In God's good time, He did address the timing of both the coming of Messiah and His kingdom. To provide such a calendar the Lord prepared one of the wisest men of unblemished character in the Old Testament. His name, of course, was Daniel, and it is to his unique contribution to Old Testament prophecy that we must address.

GOD SET HIS TIMECLOCK

Though the Bible is not a "Farmer's Almanac," it is not just a hodgepodge of apocalyptic drama either. Its prophecies have a neatly programmed calendar, set on a countdown schedule. We live in a time-space universe, and God has taught us to keep time. He is the author of time. In the outworking of His program, He is not nervously watching the cycles of history, hoping to somehow slip in His predicted agenda. His calendar for the future is precise, worked out before the world began.

This divine timetable, however, is not open for public inspection. It is more like a family secret, made known to those in the family who can be trusted with it. That presumption may irk the unbelieving world, but His program is with people of faith, not those who reject His Word.

Daniel's Uniqueness as a Prophet

Such a man of mettle was Daniel the prophet. He was, in fact, one of the finest men of sterling character in the Old Testament. Only Joseph parallels him in moral fiber and spiritual resolve. Both were disciplined by severe trials in foreign lands, and both learned to stand alone with God. The Lord seldom uses anyone who is not willing to purify his life, and these were outstanding examples of that principle. Like Joseph, Daniel rose to a pinnacle of power in world empires. Several times he served as prime minister, both over Babylon and Persia, thus exerting immense influence in world affairs.

Daniel's most significant role, of course, was that of a prophet. In line with his royal genealogy and background, his prophecies deal with Gentile kings and empires, primarily as they relate to Israel. The events of those empires took on great importance in prophecy, for God used them to peg significant points in His future program for both Israel and the world. On God's prophetic timeclock, these Gentile nations serve as hour hands, indicating to Israel and all God's people the time and progress of His program.

Daniel's prophecy is different from the other Major Prophets in that he has very little to say of Messiah. On only two occasions does he refer to Messiah, once as being "cut off" (9:25–26), and once as a crushing "stone" that comes to set up an everlasting kingdom (2:44–45). But his emphasis is more on Antichrist, who stalks as a shadowy figure throughout the book and whose demonic agents seek to control empires (Daniel 10:13, 20). Daniel's concern is to trace the movement of empires and international affairs. He seeks to alert the godly of Israel to an awareness of God's sovereignty in world affairs, recording the repeated testimony of stubborn King Nebuchadnezzar that God reigns supreme in the kingdoms of men (Daniel 2:47; 3:29; 4:35).

His main concern, then, is with the movement of Gentile kings and kingdoms who inadvertently serve God's purposes, in spite of themselves. Daniel outlines those movements, showing also the coming role of Antichrist who will epitomize ungodly kings. As Isaiah the prophet emphasized redemptive history, Daniel the royal statesman gives the structure of kingdom history till Messiah sets up His world Kingdom.

Daniel then develops his prophetic chronology along two

basic lines which are parallel at many points: The "times of the Gentiles" and the "Seventy Weeks for Israel." These two structures concern events on the international scene that relate to Israel, all leading to the eventual coming of God's kingdom on earth.

The Times of the Gentiles

The "times of the Gentiles" is that period of time in which the Gentiles have dominion over Israel, especially Jerusalem. It does not mean the whole history of Gentile kingdoms, but a specific series. Though the term is not used by Daniel, it was coined by our Lord as He referred to Daniel's prophecy in Luke 21:24. Jesus declared that Jerusalem would be "trampled underfoot by the Gentiles, until the times of the Gentiles be fulfilled." Therefore, this period began when Jerusalem was captured by Nebuchadnezzar in 605 B.C., and will be completed when Christ comes to set up His everlasting kingdom on earth (Daniel 1:1–2; 2:44; Luke 21:27).

Before further identifying this period, we should note what Daniel has to say about Gentile kingdoms, one of the basic themes of his book. He introduces them in chapter 2 by noting Nebuchadnezzar's dream of a great statue, representing five successive Gentile kingdoms. Through chapter 6 he elaborates on the theme of their subservience to God. In chapter 7 Daniel himself has a vision which restates the same structure of the times of the Gentiles, but from a different viewpoint. As King Nebuchadnezzar saw it in chapter 2 as a brilliant statue from the human view, Daniel the prophet saw it from the divine view as a menagerie of wild animals. That vicious character under demonic influences is then elaborated by Daniel through chapter 11. The last chapter culminates his theme by showing the divine rescue and assessment. Let's look more closely at these two pictures.

The Human View

Nebuchadnezzar's dream of a great metallic statue in Daniel 2 gives a picturesque description of the times of the Gentiles. The statue's five body parts indicate five successive world empires from its head of gold to its toes of iron and clay:

1) The head of gold—identified as Babylon;
2) The breast and arms of silver—Persia;
3) The belly and thighs of bronze—Greece (and four divisions);
4) The legs of iron—Rome;
5) The feet and toes of iron and clay—Revived Rome.

These five kingdoms were foreseen as dominating Israel during her time of disfranchisement. They would be her overlords until Messiah's rule would come. Daniel elaborates on the first and last kingdoms, especially the last. This will be a confederacy of ten kingdoms in power when Messiah comes to crush all authority and set up His everlasting kingdom. Its character of iron and clay suggests great strength, but little cohesion. The dream ends with the entire statue of Gentile empires being destroyed by a supernatural "stone" falling on its feet, that is, on the final form of Gentile rule.

Two progressions are suggested by the various metals used to symbolize these successive empires. The first is a progressive deterioration or lessening value and specific gravity of the metals. Gold is more valuable and heavier than silver, and so on down the line from the head of the statue to the toes. Similarly, the power of Babylon was concentrated in the head; that of Medo-Persia was divided; and likewise Greece and Rome more distributed. Rome, in fact, was ruled by the senate and the army, the emperor being chosen from one of these groups. In the final kingdom of iron and clay that deterioration is so wide spread as to suggest fierce independence and heterogeneity.

The second progression is that of the increased strength of the metals from gold to iron. The probable implication is that the overall strength of each succeeding empire progressively increases. Babylon, for instance, was strong, but small and insignificant compared with the universal power of Rome. Thus each of the four empires had a progressively wider rule and lasted a longer time.

The principle lesson of the great statue, however, concerns the beginning and end of the times of the Gentiles. That period began with the reign of Nebuchadnezzar, the "head of gold," and it will come to an end when the God of heaven comes to destroy Gentile rule and set up His everlasting kingdom on earth. Gentile kings rule only at the behest of God and are governmentally responsible to Him.

The Divine View

The last half of Daniel (7–12) is almost entirely prophetic, giving an increasingly concentrated picture of the end-time period. That final period will bring the times of the Gentiles to a close and usher in the everlasting kingdom of Messiah. Note how these chapters progressively focus on the end-times. Chapter 7 gives the broad outline; 8 emphasizes the rise of the middle kingdoms of Medo-Persia and Greece to develop the details of the little horn of the end-times; 9 brings Israel into the picture to show the relation of Israel's future to the times of the Gentiles; and 10–12 conclude the prophecy by highlighting the character and activities of the increasingly emerging figure of Antichrist in relation to Israel. The focus is on the end-time period when God will bring all nations to account as to how they have used or misused their authority, especially with relation to Israel.

The broad outline of chapter 7 is similar to that of chapter 2, but with some striking differences and additions. Here Daniel has the vision and the times of the Gentiles are seen from the divine view in the imagery of four scrapping beasts. All are carnivorous and prey on victims around the great sea, that is, the Mediterranean. The description of each beast suggests something of the character of the kingdom it represents. One is a lion with wings; the second, a bear standing higher on one side; the third, a leopard with four wings and heads; and the last a vicious nondescript beast with iron teeth. This last beast is seen to have ten horns, out of which an eleventh (little horn) arises to dominate all.

Daniel's focus in this vision is on the little horn, a detail not included in chapter 2. After inquiring about it, he is informed that the little horn is a final king who will arise out of a small kingdom to assume world control. Special note is made of his anti-God character and violence against the saints for a period of three and one-half years (7:20–25). This blasphemous tyrant is finally broken by the coming of the "Most High," who with the saints sets up an everlasting kingdom. The whole prophecy has a storybook ending of triumph, but the intervening period of Gentile domination is portrayed as one of much grief for the saints, especially in its final form.

The Divine Purpose

To recognize the divine purpose of this extended period of Gentile rule over Israel, it will help to recall the background that brought it about. Before Israel became a nation, many Gentile kingdoms had flourished for centuries. Most of them were idolatrous and quite independent of God (Genesis 10–11). When the Lord called Abraham and the patriarchs, He proposed to set up a national theocracy that would rule the world for God. Israel became that chosen nation, being called out of Egypt and organized to be a theocratic society. As such, Israel was responsible to bring the knowledge of God to all the world, as Solomon declared in his inaugural prayer and blessing (1 Kings 8:43,60). Had they done so, they would have been given an extended theocratic rule over the earth.

Israel, however, failed miserably in this responsibility. Besides that, she refused to subject herself to the Lord's leadership. Therefore, God sent them many chastisements, as He had promised in Leviticus 26. Instead of being warned by these, they only increased in callousness, the South failing to take heed even after the destruction of the North (Isaiah 5:4; Ezekiel 23:9–11; Hosea 6:4ff). They degenerated downward and became even worse than the heathen. In the end, contempt for God's Word came to characterize the whole nation, prophets, priests, princes, and people alike (Jeremiah 36:23–24; Ezekiel 22:25–30).

God's final response to this contempt for His authority was sharp and decisive. He sent them into exile and ended the nation's theocratic authority. Refusing to submit to God's authority, Israel was relieved of her own kingdom authority. The Lord sent Nebuchadnezzar in 605 B.C. to take Jerusalem, and Israel's king was shortly taken to Babylon in chains. The last two reigns were only caretaker roles, ending in further defiance.

This subjugation began the period known as the times of the Gentiles. It is the time in which God rules Israel through the

Gentiles, rather than using Israel to extend His rule over the world. This change in the divine economy concerning Israel and Jerusalem characterizes the entire period of the Gentiles. The first six chapters of Daniel emphasize the fact that, although Gentile rulers are on the throne, they have that authority only under the sovereign rulership of God. This point was hard for some to accept, but Nebuchadnezzar, the first king of these Gentiles, gave it as his final recorded testimony. He traumatically got the message, though it took a seven-year tutoring stint under the jack-rabbits for him to finally pass the test (Daniel 4:32–33).

Our Relation to the Times of the Gentiles

Having looked at the prominent features of this period, we might ask whether we are today living in the "times of the Gentiles." Jesus declared that "Jerusalem will be trampled underfoot by the Gentiles, until the times of the Gentiles be fulfilled" (Luke 21:24). Did that period come to a close when modern Israel recaptured Jerusalem in 1967?

Probably not. The end of that period, as noted by Daniel, is marked by Christ's coming as the "stone" to destroy Gentile rule and set up His everlasting kingdom. That is undoubtedly a future event. Furthermore, Jerusalem and its holy places are hardly in Israel's possession today, though they claim the city as their capital. For them to presume to occupy the temple square would quickly incite international jihad by the Muslims. Their claim to Jerusalem today is precarious at best.

It might also be noted that Israel's kingdom is nonexistent in the divine economy during the Church age. As Paul declares, there is "no difference" between Jews and Greeks, but all are regarded as one herd of sinners and candidates for salvation in the body of Christ (Romans 3:22; 11:32; Galatians 3:28). Although the Jews are still a chosen people, God recognizes no "kingdom" of Israel under covenant relations today. They have neither their Old covenant kingdom status nor its ritual system, as symbolized by the rent vail at Jesus' death.

The divine purpose of this Gentile calendar was to alert all to the fact that the Lord is sovereign in all the affairs of men, even those of the Gentiles. He is not just a casual or uncommitted observer. His covenant plans to establish an everlasting kingdom of righteousness on the earth are doing fine. They have not gone awry, Israel's infidelity and the Gentiles seeming upset of the divine applecart notwithstanding. In His time each of the Gentiles empires dutifully played its role, and that final empire of Antichrist is waiting in the wings to do likewise.

The Seventy Weeks of Israel: God's Jewish Timeclock
The Lord has given us more than one way to tell time. Another measurement of the progress of His program is the time cycle known as the "seventy weeks of Israel." This was also given by vision and is recorded in Daniel 9, a chapter that is peculiarly Jewish. It is the only chapter in Daniel that uses the covenant name LORD (YHWH; 8 times) or deals primarily with Israel. This timeclock has a Jewish accent, describing events on the local landscape of Israel rather than on the international scene. Though running on the current of Israel's life, it does have some similar features to the times of the Gentiles. It begins at a specific historic point, involves a series of national events, and concludes by fulfilling several important divine purposes. This timeclock constitutes the basic framework of prophecy for the nation Israel.

Background of this Prophecy

As with the vision concerning the Gentiles, this prophecy was given out of a background of national stress. The scene, again, was Babylon. Jerusalem had been destroyed and the people had been in captivity for nearly seventy years. This captivity was attributed by the prophets to the fact that Israel had cheated the Lord out of seventy sabbatic years and Jubilees. That amounted to about 490 years of disobedience, dating back to the beginning of the nation (2 Chronicles 36:21). As they were being taken to Babylon, Jeremiah had predicted they would be there for seventy years, after which they would be returned (Jeremiah 25:11; 29:10). Their time of discipline in the divine woodshed was nearly finished.

Many of the Jews in Babylon, however, had settled down and taken on the style of the "good life" in that prosperous river valley. Still others, such as Daniel, had their eyes on Mt. Zion in Jerusalem and God's promise to bring about a return. The high positions Daniel attained in Babylon had not spoiled his spiritual vision. As he studied Jeremiah's prophecy of return in 537, he sensed the urgency of the time and sought the Lord in confession and supplication. This, by the way, was shortly after his being cast into the lion's den for his faithfulness in prayer in chapter 6.

Far from demanding that God fulfill His promises to return His people, Daniel recognized that God works only through repentant people; He responds to those who humbly seek His mercies (9:118). The prophet perceived that God rarely does anything without first moving His people to desperate prayer. He moves people before moving mountains—or empires. Accordingly, Daniel's study of Scripture moved him to pray, and his prayer moved God to act.

The Lord's response at this time, however, was not what might have been expected. Instead of dispatching the archangel Michael to fetch all the strays back to Jerusalem, He sent Gabriel on a prophecy mission. God was about to enact a fresh program in Israel before He would fulfill His covenant promises. With Israel's seventy years captivity drawing to a close, there would indeed be a return to the homeland. But another period of "seventy" lay before the nation—not seventy years, but seventy "weeks" (shavua), that is seventy "sevens" or 490 years. Those 490 would also be divided into three divisions: seven sevens (49), sixty-two sevens (434), and one seven (7) (Daniel 9:24–27) to fulfill the cycle.

Purpose of the Seventy Weeks for Israel

The evidence is that Daniel and others of the Jewish captives looked for more than just a hike back to Jerusalem. Many were concerned for their spiritual needs and God's promises. They looked for Messiah and the inauguration of His messianic kingdom, as foretold in the Scriptures. Those anticipations are implied in Daniel 9:24, and they constitute the major divine purposes which the Lord will fulfill at the conclusion of the seventy weeks. These may be summarized in seven points:

1) The overall purpose: to fulfill the covenants with Israel.
2) The social purpose: to end Israel's transgression of the Law.
3) The redemptive purpose: to make final atonement for sin.
4) The reconciling purpose: to achieve reconciliation with God.
5) The kingdom purpose: to establish the kingdom of righteousness.

6) The prophetic purpose: to seal or complete prophecy.
7) The glory purpose: to anoint the "most holy" (i.e., prepare the temple for the return of the "Glory").

Whether all these things were understood or even anticipated, they were promised by the prophets and are listed here by
Gabriel as things that should have been expected (9:21–24). The
angel declared that, after a period of seventy sevens, all these
divine purposes would be fulfilled.

For Daniel and the faithful of Israel this vision provided an
answer to two baffling mysteries that would concern them in the
coming centuries. The first was the question of when Messiah
would come to deal with sin and when He would set up His kingdom on earth. This showed that those events were yet in the
distant future. The second was the question of how the changes
of world empires would relate to Israel and her future. This
prophecy showed that God's timeclock is geared to both the international scene and to specific events in Israel. They also showed
their relation to the prophecies of Isaiah and the other Prophets.

Beginning of the Seventy Weeks

This Jewish time schedule is much more precise than that of the
"times of the Gentiles." It is almost a digital clock. It's purpose was
to mark off specific segments of time and events to instruct those
anticipating God's program. As a time devise, it had specific mark-
ings to indicate its starting point so that the projected time
schedule would not be in doubt. Its starting point was the time of
"the issuing of a decree to restore and rebuild Jerusalem" (Daniel
9:25). That rebuilding is further delineated to be the building of
the street and wall of Jerusalem.

This starting point is often debated, however, inasmuch as several decrees were issued by Gentile rulers relative to the exiles' return (Ezra 1:1–2; 6:3, 13; Nehemiah 2:1–6). Only one, however, answers the description of this prophecy concerning rebuilding the city wall. That is the decree of the Persian emperor, Artaxerxes Longimanus, who sent Nehemiah back to Jerusalem specifically to rebuild the city wall (Nehemiah 2:1–6). For the remnant of Israel, that date was most memorable, for that decree allowed them finally to gain a semblance of independence and protection against the continued onslaughts of their neighbors (Nehemiah 6:15). Nehemiah's record of this date is also quite precise (Nisan 1, 444 B.C.), establishing a firm point of beginning for this Jewish calendar of seventy weeks.

Sixty-nine Weeks Until Messiah

The first focal point of this prophecy is the coming of "Messiah the Prince." The time span till that event is given as 483 years, or two segments of seven sevens and sixty-two sevens. The first seven (49 years) evidently spoke of the "troublous times" of rebuilding Jerusalem from 444 to 395 B.C. That period also saw the conclusion of the Old Testament prophets, which was the start of the 400 years of prophetic silence till the coming of John the Baptist.

The question is often asked: "by what interpretive hocus-pocus do we get seven years out of one "week"? The answer is that the term "week" (Heb. shavua; Gr. heptad) simply means "seven"; whether it speaks of days or years is determined by the context. That same term is used in Genesis 29:27 of Jacob's seven years service to obtain Rachael. In the context of Daniel 9, the prophet had just studied Jeremiah's prophecy of Israel's seventy years captivity, a punishment for failing to keep sabbatical and Jubilee years for

490 years (2 Chronicles 36:21). Thus this additional period of 490 years of trial under the gentiles fits the context. The "sixty-nine weeks" then designates a total of 483 years till "Messiah the Prince," beginning with the command to rebuild Jerusalem in Nisan 1, 444 B.C.

The Time of Messiah's Coming

The point at which the sixty-nine weeks (483 years) ended has also been a matter of controversy among interpreters. Various methods of calculating that span have been used. Perhaps the most precise is that of adding up the number of Bible years and days (360 days to a year, Genesis 7:11, 24; 8:4; Revelation 11:3; 12:6; 13:5); and then measuring them out on the actual calendar of solar years (a solar year being 365.24217 days, or 365 days, 5 hours, 48 min. and 46 sec.). This may be outlined as follows:

1) Total Bible days: 69 x 7 = 483 yrs. x 360 days=173,880 days.
2) Actual Solar years: 173,880 - 365.24217 days= 476.0677 years.
3) Total time span: Nisan 1, 444 B.C. + 476.0677 yrs.= Mar.30, A.D. 33.
4) Check: Nisan 1, 444 B.C. to Ni. 1 (Mar. 5), 33 A.D. = 476 years.
   Add .0677 yrs. x 365.24217 = 24.726 days= March 30, 33 A.D.

That date, March 30, A.D. 33, was Palm Sunday, the day Jesus entered Jerusalem as "the King who comes in the name of the Lord" (Psalm 118:26; Luke 19:38). The prophet Zechariah had also referred to it as the day "your King is coming to you…riding on a donkey" (Zechariah 9:9). Later that day Jesus wept over the city, announcing its coming destruction. The reason He gave: "because you did not know the time of your visitation" (Luke 19:42, 44). He sharply rebuked them for not knowing the prophetic significance of Messiah's coming on that day—the day Daniel's prophecy of the sixty-nine weeks came to an end.

If these calculations are correct, the scientific accuracy of this prophecy is remarkable, and for many, unbelievable. But why should we think it incredible that "God should raise the dead" or demonstrate His sovereign accuracy? Although He does not give us prophecy to entertain our curiosity, He does give it to strengthen our sense of His sovereignty in all things.

EVENTS FOLLOWING THE SIXTY-NINE WEEKS

Besides the good news of Messiah's coming, the angel Gabriel had some jolting news for Israel. Two tragedies would follow Messiah's arrival. The first was that this Anointed One would be cut off after His initial appearance. Far from receiving His kingdom and establishing world rule, He would be struck down, not receiving His due. This, of course, accords with Isaiah's revelation of the Suffering Servant in Isaiah 53, and Zechariah's mention of His piercing (12:10). That they fully understood it is doubtful, but the Lord intimated that they should have had some awareness of it.

The second tragedy revealed to Daniel was the consequent destruction of the holy city and the desecration of the temple. With the city and temple not even rebuilt following its first destruction, the angel predicted another destruction, followed by an extended period of war and desolation. Jesus likewise foretold this destruction, with an added announcement: the Jewish people

would soon be all but decimated, and those remaining would be
taken captive into all the world (Luke 21:24). That destruction we
know took place in A.D. 70 in the aftermath of a Jewish revolt and
two-year siege of the city by the Romans. So devastating was this
leveling of the city, there was little more than ashes and corpses
that remained. An exception was part of the Western Wall (Wailing Wall), which was spared as a warning to any future rebels who
might challenge the power of Rome. Furthermore, the plight of
the surviving Jews became even worse than slavery as they were
humiliated and used for lion fodder in the arenas of dispersion
throughout the world. The enormity of these two tragedies for the
nation are beyond calculation.

Is There a Gap in the Seventy Weeks?

The fact that these two tragedies were to take place after Messiah's
appearance suggests the need to recognize a gap between the
sixty-ninth and seventieth weeks. Not that Daniel's prediction
made such a gap necessary, but the events of history show that a
gap was, in fact, introduced. Though there are many who deny
this, several considerations make such an extended hiatus obvious. The first is that there was a gap of nearly forty years between
Jesus' death and the destruction of Jerusalem, as predicted by
Gabriel. If a short gap did indeed take place, what would militate
against a longer one?

Secondly, Jesus Himself saw the seventieth week as future,
declaring that the "abomination of desolation" spoken of by
Daniel would occur shortly before His second coming (Daniel
9:27; 12:11; Matthew 24:15, 21). That event would, in fact, be a
sign of His soon return. He thus evidently assumed a giant gap
between the sixty-ninth and seventieth weeks.

Finally, if the seventieth week did follow immediately after the sixty-ninth and no gap was intended, where then are the things that should have been fulfilled at the end of the seventy weeks? Where are the "finish of transgressions" by the people and the kingdom of "everlasting righteousness" that should have followed?

It is therefore evident that a gap did occur after the sixty-ninth week and that this Jewish timeclock stopped when Messiah was cut off. In God's good time it will be reactivated to fulfill the seventieth week. That future resumption will take place after the present age of the church is finished and the Lord again begins to deal with Israel as His covenant people. Until that time, that covenant clock has lost its tick, and although repairmen are busy clearing out the cobwebs today, it is still idle as a timepiece.

The Beginning of the Seventieth Week for Israel

Daniel's prophecy gave a specific time when that clock would again be plugged in to measure off the final seven years. That will be when the "coming prince" makes a covenant with the nation Israel (Daniel 9:27). This alliance will be made for a period of seven years, though the pact will be broken at midpoint by a change of character in the coming prince.

We immediately ask: "Who is this prince, and how is he a prince?" Also, why would he make a covenant with Israel?

He is identified here simply as one that comes from the same origin as the people who would later destroy Jerusalem (9:26). Since that was Rome, this unnamed prince evidently comes from some section of the old Roman Empire. Daniel's reference to him as "the prince that shall come," also implies that he is a figure already referred to in his prophecies. In chapter 7 this mysterious bogeyman is seen as the "little horn," and in chapter 8, as the "king of fierce countenance." He was to appear in the latter time and would oppose the "Prince of princes" (8:23–25). The one he describes is doubtless the Antichrist who will arise in the end-time as the destroyer of God's people. His being the fierce king of Syria and also from the Roman Empire does not constitute a problem, for Syria was part of the old Roman Empire. The term "prince" means a ruler or leader, not just the son of a sovereign.

The second question is why Antichrist would make a covenant with Israel? Some suggestive clues are here given as to the content of that covenant. The fact that it is broken at the mid-point, halting the "sacrifice and oblation," is really the key. This implies that Israel's old ritual system will have been reinstituted prior to this time, before it is suddenly stopped. Evidently the Antichrist will have made a seven-year treaty with Israel, allowing her to reinstitute and carry on her sacrificial system.

For that to happen further implies that a temple of sorts will have been built on the old Temple Mount (perhaps north of the present Dome of the Rock which archaeologists now believe is misplaced some 340 feet south of the original altar). Israel's offerings and rituals cannot be resumed without such a temple on that spot. That, however, would incur worldwide Muslim wrath, since that is part of Islam's Haram es Sherif or "Noble Sanctuary." It is therefore evident that the Antichrist will begin with some kind of concessions to allow Israel to set up her ritual system.

The Time of Abomination and Desolation

For some reason, however, this whimsical dictator will break that alliance with Israel after the first three and a half years, calling a halt to their sacrificial rites. This will be a turning point event that will commence a period of great trial for the Jews, unprecedented in the history of mankind (Daniel 12:1). Daniel describes it as a time of abomination and desolation, the altar abominated and the people desolated. He later reveals that the Antichrist will magnify himself in the place of God and reign supreme for three and one-half years. Only by the help of the archangel Michael will the remnant of Israel be preserved through this holocaust. Many will be tried and purified, Daniel declares, but the wicked will only become more wicked.

The reason this covenant is broken at the midpoint is not revealed by Daniel, but is strongly suggested in other passages. Ezekiel 38–39 gives the political reasons, for instance, and John in Revelation 12–13 shows the supernatural causes. The significance of this broken covenant and its aftermath will be seen to be cataclysmic for the nation, but essential to God's program to bring in everlasting righteousness.

SUMMARY

This brief review of Daniel shows the importance of his two major themes, the times of the Gentiles and the seventy weeks of Israel. Those prophecies put God's program on a careful time schedule, pegging future events for both world empires and the people of Israel. It alerted the faithful of Israel to the fact that the covenant Lord was still sovereign in world affairs, though wickedness seemed to rule.

That vision was most important to the buffeted remnant in the coming centuries when evil empires governed the land and the cause of righteousness seemed all but lost. Though silent and incognito, the Lord still ruled "within the shadows, keeping watch above His own." "Behold, He that keeps Israel will neither slumber

nor sleep" (Psalm 121:4). The covenant Lord would not desert
His chosen heritage, even in dispersion.

When Messiah did come in the passage of time, He came to
fulfill those covenant promises and prophecies. He came as the
long-anticipated Deliverer. Nonplussed, we naturally ask: "Why
were those many promises of messianic glory not fulfilled?" What
went wrong at Messiah's first coming to His people? And what
went right?

THE PSALMS
INCLUDE
HIS COMING

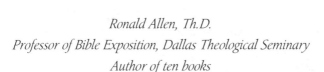

Ronald Allen, Th.D.
Professor of Bible Exposition, Dallas Theological Seminary
Author of ten books

But where is the song? When you think of biblical prophecy, what do you think of first?

Do you think of elaborate charts and tables? Do you think of ghastly creatures and horrid images? Does the phrase "biblical prophecy" cause you to think of the books of Daniel and Revelation or of the popular writers on prophetic themes? Does the word "prophecy" make you think of Armageddon? Of 666? Of the beast and his prophet? Of the common market and communism? Of war and famine? Of judgment and despair?

Does the phrase "biblical prophecy" make you think of *music and song?*

The New Song

"Of song?" you ask. That's right! Among other associations you may have concerning biblical prophecy, one that is essential is the association of *song.* A significant aspect of biblical prophecy is *the new song* that will animate God's creation and fill His people when the promises of Jesus and His kingdom are realized on earth.

Not only will music and song be a part of the kingdom that is to come, but also some of the great prophecies of that kingdom are themselves given *in song*. Somewhat unexpectedly, we find major texts on biblical prophecy in the Book of Psalms. As Psalms, these texts are musical settings. Here I am not thinking so much of the Messianic Psalms, as they are usually described. Instead, I have in mind those Psalms which speak of the *rule* or reign of God, both in the present and in the future kingdom. Many of these Psalms, in fact, have the expression "the Lord reigns." A common—and very appropriate—designation for these Psalms is "the Royal Psalms."

We've Lost the Music

When was the last time you heard a prophetic message that spoke of the music and song of the kingdom of Christ? We often find ourselves so taken up with details of interpretation, debates about chronology, and decisions respecting figures of speech that we seem to be quite unaware of the *music* of biblical prophecy. In many of the Psalms of the Hebrew Scriptures we have prophecy and music together. This is music we need to hear.

Some of the music of these prophetic Psalms is in a major key, with strong rhythms and bold themes. These Psalms include 98, 93, and 99. Prophecy, in other words, is a major theme.

There is also music of the prophetic Psalms that is in a minor key and is unexpected and unpredictable, lamentive but still expectant. Examples include Psalms 10, 60, and 14.

There is a biblical music of prophecy that is martial and strident, with harsh harmonies—all drums and brass. Look at Psalms 2, 97, and 110.

Further, you can find a prophetic music that is truly majestic, genuinely beautiful and fulfilling—with which the universe will one day resound. A splendid example is the Psalm found in Isaiah 12. These varied musical experiences should be shared by us all.

As you read and study these varied Psalms you can look for their message as well as their mood, for information as well as for attitude. You can listen to the *music*.

Back to the Psalms

As we think of biblical prophecy in the Psalms, there are two impressions we should avoid. One danger is for us to expect too much. The Psalms, for example, have nothing specific to say concerning the identification of the beast in Revelation. Nor do the Psalms say anything respecting the dating sequence of the rapture and the tribulation. Most certainly, the Psalms do not pinpoint the date of the return of the Lord.

Another danger in reading the Psalms for prophecy is to expect too little. For the Psalms do present considerable detail respecting the coming of God's kingdom on earth, the battle of Armageddon, and the glory of the King who is to come. In addition, the Psalms have an uncanny ability to present the tensions believers face as they live in the age of expectancy—for example, the onslaught of the enemies of God versus His righteousness.

Let me say it as boldly and plainly as I know how. It is time we get our hope in the Second Coming of Christ fastened into our *worship and adoration* of the Triune God. Prophecy is not given as brain food for a speculative head trip where dazzling facts are assembled for a gnostic astroprojection into the events of the future. Instead, the prophetic word calls us to worship God for His promised salvation, and to live holy lives.

Hymnic Distinctives

As we think of prophecy in the Psalms, we are reminded of the distinctives of this part of our Bible.[1]

The Psalms are poetry. It is not sufficient merely to give assent to the poetic character of the Psalms for them to have their way in us. We need to *read* the Psalms as poems (and I encourage you to read them aloud in your personal daily worship). In these poems of the Bible we find many of the conventions of secular poetry. An Italian sonnet and a Japanese Haiku share a poetic spirit with a Hebrew Psalm. But the Psalms of the Bible are distinct in form and in image, in theology and in purpose.

The material form of the biblical poems is termed *parallelism.* Statement is followed by restatement, and these elements are to be heard together as they enhance one another. Read the following lines from the intensely prophetic Psalm 24 and see how this works.

> The earth is the LORD's, and all its fullness,
> The world and those who dwell therein (v. 1).
>
> Who may ascend into the hill of the LORD?
> Or who may stand in His holy place? (v. 3).
>
> Lift up your heads, O you gates!
> And be lifted up, you everlasting doors!
> And the King of Glory shall come in (v. 7).
>
> Who is this King of glory?
> The LORD strong and mighty,
> The LORD mighty in battle (v. 8).

I like to compare the poetry of the Bible to music heard through a stereophonic music system. The sounds of one speaker blend with and enhance the sounds of the other speaker. Condensed editions of the Scriptures often cut parallel lines. One should no more think of dropping a parallel line of Hebrew poetry than one would think of shutting off one channel of a stereo recording. We should listen to the two lines together in the same way that we listen to the two tracks of stereo music. The words of one line play with the words of the other to create an impression that is grander than either statement alone.

As we approach a poem in the Bible, we should not atomize the poem by looking at each verse as an individual unit. The poems of the Bible are written in movements or strophes, sections that correspond to a paragraph of prose. In the shorter Psalms we often find two, three, or four movements; some have considerably more. Some Psalms have obvious markers for these movements; in others the movements are more subtle. But we should look for internal indicators of structure as significant interpretive keys to the poet's idea.

In the poems of the Bible we find imagery that is distinctive to the Old Testament world. Some of the imagery in the Bible is transparent and common to world literature. Pastoral imagery is not limited by time. But some of the poems in the Bible use images that need to be explained to the modern reader, as they are based on cultural issues that were distinctive to a given time and place.

The Canaanite concept of Baal, for example, for the poets of the Bible took particular delight in using figures of speech from Canaanite poetry which they then applied to Yahweh, God of Israel. In this way they both glorified God and debunked Baal.

The most important gain for us in learning to recognize the poetic cast of the Psalms is to be prepared to *experience* what these poems present. Poetry is the most compressed form of literature, and—when read correctly—may be experienced the most keenly. We do not just hunt for a message in the Psalms; we are moved by the Psalms as we learn to experience the message that they describe.

The Psalms are music. Not only are the Psalms recognized as poetry, they are viewed as music. They are Hebrew songs of worship and praise. These old poems which we now read and study were once the lyrics of songs. Many people still sing them. Some Christians sing the Psalms in the musical settings established early in the Reformation. One communion, for example, sings the Psalms exclusively in English metrical patterns set to Genevan hymn tunes. Others sing these songs in musical settings that are very new and contemporary. Maranatha! Music has produced an album of Psalms in the idiom of contemporary praise music.[2] Some talented musicians in the church sing the Psalms in extemporaneous song; many Jewish people sing the Psalms in traditional chants.

But however they are used, the Psalms beg to be sung. *The Psalms are music.* And the fact that they are music directs us to the active admiration and adoration of the Lord. The Psalms were sung in the worship services in the temple in ancient Israel. The Psalms were sung in incantation by the early Christians in their worship meetings. The Psalms have been adapted to nearly every taste and style of music used by the church throughout its history. If we learn to sing these old songs we will find ourselves prompted to have the proper response to God as we live in an increasingly hostile age.

The Psalms are relevant. The Psalms are poems and they are music. They are also relevant. The Psalms do not exist to fulfill our prophetic curiosity. The Psalms are designed to relate to our everyday lives, even as they met the needs of the believers in ancient Israel. They speak to us where we are and as we are. They *live*.

Following a sermon, a speaker is sometimes told that he has made the Bible passage used in the message come alive. We understand the good intentions behind such statements. But we strive to make a more accurate impression. The Bible *does live* (see Hebrews 4:12); life is not something that we bestow upon it when we present it well. Rather, when one presents the message of the Bible in a relevant way, we allow the Bible to demonstrate the life that it has.

My beloved professor of homiletics (preaching), Dr. Haddon Robinson, used to tell us that it is a sin to bore people with the Word of God.

It should come as no surprise that the message of the text of Scripture is a living message. We should expect to see its life. When a speaker becomes an obstruction between the text and his listeners, the life of the Scriptures is hidden.

Of all the Old Testament books, the life of the Bible is seen most clearly in the Psalms. By learning to read the Psalms as poems and to appreciate them as music, we find that the Psalms demonstrate their life and relevance most clearly to the modern reader.

The Psalms are prophetic. Not all of the Psalms are centrally prophetic, and certainly not all of the Psalms are prophetic in the same way—but they *are* prophetic. Even the most casual reader of Psalm 110 must come to this conclusion.

Our Lord and His disciples were united in seeing the prophetic aspects of the Psalms of their ancestors. In the early preaching of the church witnessed by the Book of Acts, we find that the Psalms were used as readily as Isaiah and Joel as prophetic texts—and this despite the poetic and musical values we have already observed.[3]

At times Christ and His disciples seemed to go out of their way to stress the prophetic nature of the Psalms. Jesus quoted from Psalm 78 so that "it might be fulfilled which was spoken by the prophet" (Matthew 13:35). The "prophet" here was the psalmist! Our Lord also spoke in reference to David's prophecy in Psalm 110 (see Matthew 22:43–46; Mark 12:35–37; Luke 20:41–44) and in Psalm 2. A characteristic apostolic opinion of the prophetic nature of the Psalms is found in Acts 4:25: "You spoke by the Holy Spirit through the mouth of your servant, our father David" (NIV).

In your reading of the Psalms, I trust that you will respond to the Psalms in a variety of ways. Since the Psalms are *poetry*, we should learn to experience this art more fully. Since the Psalms are *music,* we should allow the Psalms to aid us in our worship of the Lord together. Since the Psalms are *life-related*, we may apply the teachings of these poems to our own living. And since the Psalms are *prophetic*, we have ample warrant to study Bible prophecy as it is presented.

Some Cautions

There are some aspects of the study of biblical prophecy that call for caution on our part. For some reason, which I honestly do not understand, there often seems to be a great deal of private interpretation, even nuttiness, associated with the study of the prophetic Scriptures. This observation is not concerned exclusively with the study of the Psalms, but with prophecy in general.

The great book that concludes our Bible begins with a significant blessing to those who read it rightly: "Blessed is the one who reads the words of this prophecy, and blessed are those who hear it and take to heart what is written in it, because the time is near" (Revelation 1:3 NIV). Despite the promise of blessings one should expect in the study of biblical prophecy, there is the potential danger of a curse as well. The verse just quoted speaks not only of reading but also of hearing and taking to heart. Some seem only to read (and not very well), and then go out to deceive God's people with their errors. They make no adjustments in their lives by way of response to God's prophetic word. In my opinion, no part of the Scriptures has been so regularly abused as the prophetic portions.

Some cautions that we need to observe in the study of biblical prophecy are as follows:

Professionalism. As with any topic, biblical or secular, there is a danger of one becoming so familiar with the material that it ceases to make an impression on one's life. This is "professionalism" in a negative sense. This type of thing sometimes happens when a person begins his or her study with great enthusiasm. But in time the keen edge is lost; and the study of biblical prophecy becomes simply something one does, not something to which one relates.

Sensationalism. A second area for caution in the study of biblical prophecy concerns sensationalism. There are some speakers on prophetic themes who seem to feel that the only way they will get an audience is to shock their hearers with outrageous concepts. Just a few years ago, for example, there were those who were attempting to prove that the United States secretary of state bore a name with the numerical equivalent of the mysterious "666" of Revelation 13:18.[4]

Those of us who teach the Word of God ought to be alert to the potential of confusing our own foolishness with the words of Scripture. A reading of Revelation 13 presents a picture of the beast that is so evil that I find it hard to imagine how well-meaning men could be guilty of the terrible slander of asserting that a certain person is the beast. This practice may be a crowd-pleaser; it can hardly please the Lord.

Isolationism. Yet another danger in the study of the prophetic Scriptures is to retreat from life—to leave both gainful employment and personal witness in order to "await" the second coming. Such an attitude seems to have been present from the time of the early church, and it is often observed today.

There are, by the way, even Jewish isolationists who await the coming of the messiah. The people who were responsible for the Dead Sea Scrolls were isolationists. They retreated from their society and prepared themselves for the advent of the age to come following the final battle. There are Jewish isolationists today as well. The Jewish inhabitants of Mea Shearim in Jerusalem have produced a Jewish ghetto in the holy city. They reject the present state of Israel because it was not established by the rule of the messiah, for whom they wait.

Among both Christians and Jews there are those who argue for a withdrawal from society and a denial of activity. Paul wrote to Christians with stern language:

We hear that some among you are idle. They are not busy; they are busybodies. Such people we command and urge in the Lord Jesus Christ, to settle down and earn the bread they eat. And as for you, brothers, never tire of doing what is right (2 Thessalonians 3:11–13 NIV).

Martin Luther is reported to have said that if he *knew* that the return of the Lord were tomorrow, he would plant a tree today. As we anticipate the return of Christ, we should try to live useful lives until He comes.

Disobedience. A fourth danger in the study of biblical prophecy is disobedience. This is seen particularly with respect to dating the return of Christ. The Bible does present an active sense of anticipation; it is right to expect the return of Christ in one's lifetime. But it is not right to predict the date! It is in fact disobedience to Christ (see Matthew 24:36). To say that our Lord said only that we may not know the day or the hour, but that we may know the month, is sophistry unbecoming a servant of the Lord! If ever there was an application of Aesop's story of the mischievous shepherd boy who called, "Wolf! Wolf!" it is in those students of the prophetic Scriptures who shout "The Lord will return on Tuesday!"

Presumption. One more item calls for caution—it is the presumption that we know everything there is to know about biblical prophecy. If any study of the Bible ought to drive one to his or her knees in humility, it is the study of prophecy (Philippians 2:9–11 is a *prophetic text!*). Yet for some reason we tend to be stronger in our pronouncements respecting the interpretation of prophecy than in many other areas of theology—areas lacking the interpretive difficulties that prophecy presents.

At seminary I have taught a course on the Dead Sea Scrolls. As we study some of the prophetic texts written by ancient Jewish commentators some students have inquired how those sectarians could speak with such certainty in their interpretations of difficult texts (interpretations that have been proved wrong by the passage of time). One student observed that the arrogant confidence some of us display in our reading of prophetic texts may lead to similar disappointment.

ON WITH THE MUSIC

But enough of these negative elements. Music, maestro! Hear these verses, selected from one of the poems of the Bible that calls for a new song. As you read these words, note how the Psalm progresses in three movements. This poem calls for a new song among all peoples; it does so on the basis of the rule of the Lord and the keen anticipation that *He who is King is coming.*

Psalm 96

I. Oh, sing to the LORD *a new song!*
> Sing to the LORD, all the earth.
Sing to the LORD, bless His name;
Proclaim the good news of His
> salvation from day to day.
Declare His glory among the nations,
His wonders among all peoples.
For the LORD is great
> and greatly to be praised;
He is to be feared above all gods.
For all the gods of the peoples are idols,
But the LORD made the heavens.
Honor and majesty are before Him;
Strength and beauty are in His sanctuary.

II. Give to the LORD,
> kindreds of the peoples,
Give to the LORD glory and strength.

Give to the LORD the glory due His name;
Bring an offering,
    and come into His courts.
Oh, worship the LORD in the beauty of holiness!
Tremble before Him, all the earth.
Say among the nations,
    "The LORD reigns;
The world also is firmly established,
It shall not be moved;
He shall judge the peoples righteously."

III. Let the heavens rejoice,
        and let the earth be glad;
    Let the sea roar, and all its fullness;
    Let the field be joyful,
        and all that is in it.
    Then all the trees of the wood
        will rejoice before the LORD.
    For He is coming,
        for He is coming to judge the earth.
    He shall judge the world with righteousness,
    And the peoples with His truth (emphasis added).

All nations and peoples are called upon in this Psalm to join in the *new song* of the Book of Psalms, a song of joy before our King. This Psalm is an example of the Royal Psalms, as it centers on the rule of God: "Yahweh reigns!" God is king *now,* and He is the king *who is to come,* bringing righteous judgment to the earth. All people are to respond to Him, for He is the only God, the creator of all that is. All people are to praise Him, for glory is due His name.

In the reading of this Psalm, did you listen for the mood as well as for the message? Did you listen to the music? In the Royal Psalms of the Bible we find prophecy and music holding hands. Here we find the song.

1. Considerable space was given to this discussion in the first half of my book *Praise! A Matter of Life and Breath* (Nashville: Thomas Nelson, 1980), chs. 1–7.

2. *Psalms Alive* (Costa Mesa: Maranatha! Music, MM0097, 1982) was based in part on the hymnic ideas developed in *Praise!* The composers and writers were Tom Howard, Bill Batstone, and Dori Howard. Chuck Fromm developed the concepts of a worshiping community of singers and praisers united in adoring God by linking the old words of the Psalms with the new praise music idiom of the 1980s.

3. Witness, for example, Peter's famed sermon on Pentecost (Acts 2:14–36) in which the apostle uses Psalm 16:8–11 and Psalm 110:1 with the same prophetic authority as he does Joel 2:28–32.

4. There is a whimsical note in *Eternity* (November 1982, p. 64) that shows that one can make any name total 666 to identify a potential antichrist.

THE PROMISES
TO ISRAEL PREDICT
HIS COMING

JOHN F. WALVOORD

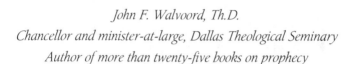

John F. Walvoord, Th.D.
Chancellor and minister-at-large, Dallas Theological Seminary
Author of more than twenty-five books on prophecy

For a Gentile believer of the twentieth century, prophecy concerning the future of Israel may seem unimportant. However, from a prophetic perspective, the future of Israel is very important. In fact, the prophecies about Israel form the background of understanding prophecy as a whole.

One of the main causes for current confusion in understanding prophecy is the failure to take Israel-related prophecies literally. Attempts to transfer the promises relating to Israel to the church have been a major obstacle to understanding God's prophetic purposes as a whole. Once prophecies about Israel are distinguished from prophecies concerning the church or the Gentiles, the main programs of God as outlined in prophecy begin to be clear.

We can see from the analysis of Old Testament prophecy that a pattern of literal fulfillment has been established. The promise to Adam and Eve of death for disobedience was literally fulfilled. The promise of salvation, first revealed to Adam and Eve, has also unfolded in history and had its climax in the death and resurrection of Christ. The predictions of the Flood and the covenant with Noah also came to dramatic and literal fulfillment. The Abrahamic covenant, in its broad provisions as originally outlined to Abraham, has, in general, already been completely fulfilled in that Abraham became a great man who had many descendants. The line of the Messiah leading to Mary has unfolded. In all of these predictions and their fulfillment, the principle of literal fulfillment of prophecy has been confirmed.

Though there is general recognition that many of the promises given to Abraham have had literal fulfillment, the question as to whether there is yet a future for Israel as a nation is a matter of dispute principally between the amillennial and the premillennial interpretation. The amillennial interpretation, which does not believe in a millennial reign after the second coming of Christ, tends to deny any future literal fulfillment, though the possibility of spiritual revival in Israel in the present age is sometimes recognized. In contrast, the premillennial interpretation pictures the second coming of Christ as bringing in a kingdom of glorious release and freedom for Israel, the seating of Christ on the throne of David, Israel's occupation of the Promised Land, and Israel as the object of God's special divine grace. Accordingly, the question as to whether Israel still has a future as a nation becomes an important aspect of the interpretation of the prophetic account.

The Promise of the Future of Israel as Fulfilled

Pattern of literal fulfillment. The prediction that from the line of Abraham would come One who would be a blessing to the entire world has already been fulfilled in Christ. Additional fulfillment is found in the prophets of the Old Testament and the apostles of the New Testament as they contributed to the spiritual blessing God has bestowed on his people. The inspiration of the written Word of God is another aspect of the fulfillment of the promise of blessing. All of these factors detailing fulfilled prophecy in a literal fashion should be taken into consideration in determining whether there is a future promise to be fulfilled.

The emergence of the nation Israel. Throughout history it has become obvious that the descendants of Abraham have emerged as a nation with millions of people. In Egypt the family of seventy may have became a people of two million or more at the time of the Exodus. Though for many generations they were persecuted and reduced in number, the people of Israel today are estimated to number from 15 to 25 million inhabitants in various parts of the world. The promise that Abraham would be a father of a great nation has been given factual support in Israel's current existence in the world.

The nation Israel recognized today. Though some extremists of one kind or another attempt to explain away any literal fulfillment of the existence of Israel today, the fact is that the world as a whole has recognized Israel as a political state and has assigned her certain territories in the Middle East. The people of Israel are very conscious of their lineage, their history, their religion, and their culture, and all of this combines to make the nation Israel what it is today. Up to the present time a literal fulfillment of the promises given to Abraham has been clearly confirmed by history.

Is a Future for the Nation Israel Certain?

The question of the future of Israel is important because it determines the interpretation of so many passages of the Bible. To some, the theological arguments may seem technical, but the question simply put is whether the prophecies about Israel should be taken in their plain and natural meaning as revealing Israel's future. The debate is between the amillennial view, which claims that there is no literal Millennium after the second coming of Christ, and the premillennial position, which believes Israel has a future Millennium after this event.

The objections of amillennialism. Even a casual examination of the evidence would indicate that inasmuch as the promises to Israel have been literally fulfilled up to the present time, a continuation of this progression of fulfillment in the future may be expected. However, the amillennial view of Scripture, which denies a future Millennium after the second coming of Christ, tends to interpret prophecy in a way which voids any literal fulfillment of a future for the nation Israel. Amillennial objections take many forms, but one of their main lines of argument is the statement that the Abrahamic covenant is conditional, that the conditions have not been met, and that therefore, the Abrahamic covenant will not be fulfilled in the future.

It is true that Abraham was obedient to God when he left his homeland and went to a land that God would show him. It is also true that Abraham was obedient in a number of particulars in his walk with God. On the other hand, it is also true that he was out of the will of God when he went down into Egypt, when he suggested Eliezer as his heir, and when he wanted Ishmael as his heir. His partial unbelief in God's promises later turned to complete faith. The promises given to Abraham by their nature, however, could not be conditional in that God promised Abraham fulfillment *forever,* as is illustrated in the many promises and reiterations of the Abrahamic covenant.

It is true that partial fulfillment of the Abrahamic covenant to any one generation and God's blessing on that generation were contingent on their obedience. The history of Israel reveals that they were frequently disobedient. In fact, Israel went down to Egypt in the time of Jacob when it was questionable whether they should have taken that step. It is also clear that, after their return to their land, they departed from God, a fact that resulted in the Assyrian and Babylonian captivities. When Israel rejected Christ, they were scattered all over the world in fulfillment of God's warning concerning disobedience.

The fact is, however, that in the midst of Israel's apostasy and sin, God gave them additional revelation concerning their future restoration. The prophet Jeremiah recorded that Israel would come back to their home after seventy years of captivity in Babylon (29:10). This was literally fulfilled, though Israel at the time was in apostasy and was spiritually unprepared to fulfill God's purpose. It is also true that through Jeremiah, in the midst of Israel's apostasy, God gave promises of Israel's ultimate blessing (see 23:5–8). Also through Jeremiah the new covenant, with its promise of ultimate blessing upon Israel, was given (31:10–14). In other words, it is clear from Scripture that the certainty of the ultimate fulfillment of the prophecy was such that even Israel's apostasy would not thwart God's ultimate purpose.

The fulfillment of the promise will be realized by those who are spiritually prepared to receive it—that is, by the godly remnant at the time of the second coming of Christ. The fact that there will be a godly remnant and that God will rescue them and place them in the millennial kingdom is a matter of specific prophecy, and the disobedience of Israel as a nation will not deter God from fulfilling this prophecy in the future. In spite of these obvious evidences that there is a future for Israel, a number of objections are brought up by the amillenarian interpretation.

Amillenarians point to the judgment on Nineveh, which was predicted by Jonah but not inflicted because of their repentance, as evidence that blessing follows obedience. The answer to this, of course, is that this was not a covenant arrangement, and it is true that their deliverance for 150 years resulted from their repentance.

The judgment on Eli the priest for his sin is cited as evidence of an implied condition of obedience in connection with God's appointment of his line as the priestly line (1 Samuel 2:30; cf. Exodus 29:9; Jeremiah 18–1; Ezekiel 3:18–19). But Eli lived under the conditional Mosaic covenant.

In these illustrations it is clear that blessing followed obedience and punishment followed disobedience, but in neither of these cases is there an ultimate promise in question. In connection with God's dealings with the nations, he was free to pluck up and cast down. He was also free to discipline any one generation of Israelites, as is illustrated many times in the Old Testament, but the continuing promise was made in spite of their apostasy and sin. When God proposed that he put aside the children of Israel and start over with Moses, there was immediate reference to the fact that God had a covenant with Israel (Exodus 32:13–14), and God did not bring this judgment on Israel.

In the Old Testament the rite of circumcision is cited as a condition for blessing. This related to the individual—that is, an uncircumcised Israelite was cut off from the covenant promise— but did not alter the promise to the nation.

Amillenarians use Esau as an illustration because he was excluded from some of the promises of blessing. This again is based on a misunderstanding. God's covenant with Abraham did not promise blessing on all his descendants but only on some; and in the extension of the Abrahamic covenant, Esau and Ishmael were expressly excluded, whereas the line of blessing went from Abraham to Isaac to Jacob and on to the twelve sons of Jacob.

Sometimes amillenarians appeal to the obedience of Christ as the ultimate argument for their position. It clearly was necessary for Christ to go to the cross to provide grace in order to fulfill the promises given to Israel, but this very argument works against the amillennial contention because the final restoration of Israel does not rest on their obedience but on the grace of God. A nation that does not deserve God's blessing will receive them, much as Christians, who do not deserve God's blessings because of their imperfections, are showered with his blessings in both time and eternity.

Amillenarians offer other objections besides the conditional nature of the promises. Some amillenarians point to partial fulfillment of the promises as sufficient to answer the problem. The development of Israel into a large nation, of course, was a partial fulfillment of the promise, but this was not what the promise required, since God promised Israel blessings that would continue for eternity.

Some amillenarians hold that the promise of the land was fulfilled in the time of Solomon, but this does not explain the many references in the Major and Minor Prophets to the land as subject to yet future fulfillment. Even in Solomon's day the land was not completely possessed though much of it was put under tribute.

Accordingly, the amillennial arguments, though numerous, are based on the insupportable premise that all the promises of God are conditional or have already been fulfilled. If the promises are conditional, there would be no sure fulfillment of any prophecy, because there are always uncertainties and contingencies involved. The ultimate question is "What has God promised?" If he has predicted a future event, then there should be no question concerning its future fulfillment.

Support for the unconditional character of the Abrahamic covenant. In denial of the concept that God's covenant with Abraham is conditional, a number of reasons can be cited as support for the concept of absolute certainty of the fulfillment of God's covenants.

All agree that the Mosaic covenant was conditional—that is, its blessings were conditioned on obedience, and its judgments would follow disobedience. But the other covenants of Israel, such as the Abrahamic covenant, the Palestinian covenant, the Davidic covenant, and the new covenant, are unconditional as far as their ultimate fulfillment is concerned, even though the blessings of the covenant in any given generation may be sacrificed by disobedience. When the Abrahamic covenant is repeated in passages subsequent to its original revelation, it is declared to be eternal, and therefore, necessarily unconditional (Genesis 17:7, 13, 19; 1 Chronicles 16:16–17; Psalm 105:9–10).

Likewise, the Palestinian covenant is everlasting in its character (Ezekiel 16:60), as are the Davidic covenant (2 Samuel 7:13, 16, 19; 1 Chronicles 17:12; 22:10; Isaiah 55:3; Ezekiel 37:25) and the new covenant, which relates to Israel's future (Isaiah 61:8; Jeremiah 32:40; 50:5; Hebrews 13:20). In the nature of an eternal promise, conditions would be irrelevant, because the promise could not be eternal if contingent on obedience.

The Abrahamic covenant was subject to repetition and enlargement in subsequent Scriptures, but in none of these were the promised blessings conditioned on obedience.

The Abrahamic covenant, particularly the promise of the land, was solemnly confirmed by the shedding of blood (Genesis 15:7–21; Jeremiah 34:18). The geographic boundaries of the land were stated in Genesis 15:18–21. These promises were given at a time when Abraham was approaching God in unbelief, and it was to sustain and support what faith Abraham had that the covenant was solemnly confirmed.

The fact that circumcision was required of individuals who wanted to claim blessing under the Abrahamic covenant does not change its unconditional character. It is clear that individuals who were not circumcised were excluded from the promise. But this did not alter the fact that the promise would be fulfilled to the nation as a whole. Circumcision was a physical sign that they belonged under the covenant blessing (Genesis 17:9–14).

It is important to realize that when the covenant of Abraham was repeated to Isaac and Jacob, no conditions were mentioned. In fact, God's covenant with Isaac came at a time when he was trying to leave the land and was used as a deterrent to keep him in the Promised Land (Genesis 26:2–5). Likewise, the covenant was confirmed with Jacob as he was running away from home because of Esau (27:41–43). He also received the covenant promise without conditions (28:13–15).

As previously pointed out, even in the apostasy of Jeremiah's day, the eternal promises were not conditioned, and Jeremiah, in the midst of the apostate generation in which he lived, was given the revelation of the certain future of Israel (cf. Jeremiah 23:5–8; 30:5–11).

One of the most determinative passages on the unconditional character of the Abrahamic covenant is found in Hebrews 6:13–18:

When God made his promise to Abraham, since there was no one greater for him to swear by, he swore by himself, saying, "I will surely bless you and give you many descendants." And so after waiting patiently, Abraham received what was promised. Men swear by someone greater than themselves, and the oath confirms what is said and puts an end to all argument. Because God wanted to make the unchanging nature of his purpose very clear to the heirs of what was promised, he confirmed it with an oath. God did this so that, by two unchangeable things in which it is impossible for God to lie, we who have fled to take hold of the hope offered to us may be greatly encouraged.

In this passage God's promise to Abraham is declared to be immutable and unchangeable. His purpose is declared to be "unchanging" (v. 17). This passage is especially significant in view of the fact that the religious leaders of Israel had rejected Christ and caused his crucifixion. In spite of this fact, the book of Hebrews points out that Israel has a certain and unchangeable promise of the fulfillment of the covenant. (See chapter 8.)

Many amillenarians, having abandoned the idea that the Abrahamic covenant is conditional, now favor interpreting it non-literally. One approach is to regard Abraham's descendants, whether Israelites or other nations, as representing the church and thereby wiping out the necessity of a future for Israel.

The literal land, literal physical descendants, literal kings, and, ultimately, a literal Messiah combine to support a literal interpretation of the Abrahamic covenant. The Old Testament consistently supports a literal interpretation of the covenant, and the New Testament adds its confirming word, including the prophecy of a millennial kingdom following the Second Coming. The variety of solutions offered by the amillenarians themselves is evidence that none of their solutions really solve their problem of denying a future Millennium and a future for the nation of Israel.

The Meaning of the Name Israel

The term Israel *as used in the Scriptures.* One way to avoid the conclusion that the Abrahamic covenant is subject to future literal fulfillment involving a future for the nation Israel is to redefine the term *Israel* so that it includes the church, thus considering the promises to Israel unliteral. Some amillenarians use this approach, claiming that Israel does not have a future because her future will be fulfilled by the church composed of Jews and Gentiles.

This raises a question as to how the term *Israel* is used in the Bible itself. The terms *Israel* and *Israelite* are found approximately 2300 times in the Old Testament, and in every case they refer to those racially descended from Jacob. In the New Testament Israel is mentioned approximately 75 times. Also, Israel is referred to as *the Jews* 80 times in the Old Testament and about 170 times in the New Testament. In all of these many references, only one or two passages leave any question concerning the reference to the twelve tribes of Israel. Obviously, the burden of proof would be on anyone who suggests that the term *Israel* includes Gentiles, though it has been characteristic of amillennialism to affirm dogmatically that Israel is a synonym for the church in the present age. In the last generation, even among amillenarians, there has been a trend away from this doctrine for a number of reasons.

One of the problems faced by those who want to make the church and Israel synonymous is that though there are many promises of blessings for Israel, there are also threats of cursing, and this complicates the identification of the two. Usually amillenarians, who hold that the church is Israel, claim only the blessings. Other problems arise because of the sheer weight of the hundreds of references to Israel that obviously do not include the church. Also in Scripture Israel is constantly contrasted with other entities.

Israel contrasted with the Gentiles. In the New Testament as in the Old there are numerous messages addressed to Israel, and this continues after the institution of the church in Acts 2 (cf. Acts 3:23; 4:8, 10; 5:21, 31, 35; 21:28; et al.). In these references it is obvious that only those who are racially Israelites are included. The same is true of Paul's prayer for Israel's salvation (Romans 10:1), which he bases on the fact that he also is an Israelite.

The use of the term *Jew* beginning in the Old Testament in the book of Esther and continuing in the New Testament, clearly describes those who are Israelites and not Gentiles. This is made obvious in the distinction of 1 Corinthians 10:32, where the threefold division of the human race into (1) Gentiles, (2) Jews, and (3) the church of God makes clear that these three separate divisions continue in the present age.

In Paul's discussion of Israel's situation in his day, he points out that the Israelites have many particular privileges (Romans 9:4–5), none of which pertain to the church. Paul's fervent prayer for Israel (vv. 2–3) is another instance of the term *Israel*, referring to twelve tribes and not to Gentiles.

The New Testament also points out that while the Jews had certain privileges, Gentiles were excluded from them, as in Paul's statement in Ephesians 2:12: "Remember that at that time you were separate from Christ, excluded from citizenship in Israel and foreigners to the covenants of the promise, without hope and without God in the world." This and other passages clearly distinguish Israel from the Gentiles.

The church contrasted with unsaved Israel. Amillenarians agree that Scripture distinguishes Israel from the church, because unsaved Israelites are obviously not part of the church. If natural Israel, including the unsaved, exists apart from the church, it is impossible to transfer promises given to the nation Israel to the church, which is composed of those who are saved in the present age.

In continuance of this contrast, the New Testament speaks of a future program for Israel as distinct from God's program for the church. In the classic passage in Romans 9–11, where the apostle is tracing Israel's relationship to what he has previously discussed in the book of Romans, he raises the specific question as to whether God has cast off the nation of Israel: "I ask then: Did God reject his people? By no means! I am an Israelite myself, a descendant of Abraham, from the tribe of Benjamin. God did not reject his people, whom he foreknew" (11:1–2). God has a program for Israel that goes beyond his program in the present age for Israel as a part of the church.

Paul recognized the present lost state of many in Israel. As a nation Israel has turned from God and is not operating under God's blessing. This is illustrated in the olive tree with the natural branches, referring to Israel, broken off, and Gentiles, represented by a wild olive shoot, grafted in (Romans 11:17). Paul warns Gentiles as a group, however, that God has a future for Israel nationally and that "all Israel will be saved" (v. 26). By this he means, not that every individual will be saved spiritually, but that Israel as a nation will be delivered when the Deliverer comes from

Zion, referring to the second coming of Christ (v. 26). Sufficient for the present study are the facts that the nation of Israel and the church are contrasted and that the nation of Israel has a future.

The Scriptures also contrast spiritual Israel with Gentile Christian believers. Here the question as to whether Gentile Christians are designated as Israelites is faced squarely. Some amillenarians teach that the church takes the place of Israel completely and that both Gentiles and Israelites fulfill the promises originally given to Israel.

Of the hundreds of passages referring to Israel and to the Jews, only two or three could possibly be interpreted as confusing the Gentiles and Israel.

According to Romans 9:6, "It is not as though God's word had failed. For not all who are descended from Israel are Israel." What is being contrasted here is the difference between those in Israel who are spiritual, or believers, and those who are only natural, that is, descendants of Jacob but not believers. In each generation Israelites who are believers inherit the promises. Gentile believers are not in view.

As has been pointed out, the promises given to Abraham concerning the nation Israel are narrowed to Isaac, not Ishmael, and to Jacob, not Esau, and to the twelve sons of Jacob. Only descendants of Jacob inherit the broad promises of God relating to the nation. Among the descendants of Jacob, however, some are true believers and inherit the spiritual promises as well and the national promises. This is what Paul refers to as the election of grace (Romans 11:5–10). In the present age Israelites who are saved become part of the church, but unbelieving Israelites are lost and are declared to be blinded.

In Romans 9:25 Paul quotes Hosea 2:23, "I will call them 'my people' who are not my people; and I will call her 'my loved one' who is not my loved one." This passage had been cited as an instance where Israel and the church are viewed together and Gentiles and Jews are considered as one people. The Hosea passage, however, is contrasting Israelites who are not the Lord's people, because of their lack of faith, with those who are true Israelites who believe in God. In the Hebrew of Hosea 2:23 there is a play on words where "Not my loved one" is a translation of the Hebrew *Lo-Ruhamah* and is contrasted with "Not my people," which is a translation of the Hebrew *Lo-Ammi*. This is quoted in Romans, not to merge the Gentiles and Israel, but to serve as an application. Just as God would bless some in Israel who, before they believed in Christ, were not of true Israel, so God would bless Gentiles who were not formerly saved. It is a matter of application rather than interpretation, and there is no reason here to confuse Gentiles with Israel. However, God does deal with them in a similar way in this passage. Both Israelites who believe and Israelites who do not believe are genuine descendants of Jacob, but only those who believe are saved. And the racial distinction between Jew and Gentile is observed.

Amillenarians also cite Galatians 6:15–16 as evidence that the church can be viewed as Israel: "Neither circumcision nor uncircumcision means anything; what counts is a new creation. Peace and Mercy to all who follow this rule, even to the Israel of God." The NIV translation, however, is questionable, since the word *even* is a translation of the Greek *kai*, which normally means "and." A more accurate translation is, "and upon the Israel of God," as in the NASB, ASV, KJV, NKJV, and NRSV. What Paul is saying is that he wishes peace and mercy upon all who are believers but especially upon the Israel of God—that is, Israelites who are saved. Though the NIV translation may have pleased amillennial scholars, a grammatically correct translation would preserve the distinction between Israel and Gentiles, in keeping with dispensational and premillennial teaching.

If the passages in Romans 9 and Galations 6 are considered in light of hundreds of passages where the word *Israel* is distinctly a reference to the descendants of Jacob, the overwhelming evidence is in favor of maintaining this distinction. Even if the amillennial interpretation is upheld, it still does not generate a broad principle that any promise given to Israel can be claimed by the church or that the promises given to Israel are canceled. Even amillenarians tend to avoid this conclusion in current literature.

Have the promises to the nation Israel been canceled? It should be clear from the historical evidence that, up to the present, God has faithfully kept his promises to Israel. Israel is still a great nation and is still blessed by God. Through Israel the Messiah has come, and many of the blessings promised have already been fulfilled. The question that remains is whether there is any scriptural evidence that Israel has been cast aside.

As pointed out briefly, the evidence of Romans 11 is to the contrary, where Paul promises a future for Israel as a nation. A few passages, however, should be considered as possibly teaching that Israel has been cast aside. In Matthew 21:43, referring to the rejection of Christ by his generation, Christ said, "Therefore I tell you that the kingdom of God will be taken away from you and given to a people who will produce its fruit." What is meant by the principal terms "kingdom of God" and "a people who will produce its fruit"? Matthew mainly uses the term "kingdom of heaven," but here is one of the few references to the "kingdom of God." In Matthew as well as other New Testament writings, the kingdom of God always refers to holy angels or people who are saved. The program of salvation, therefore, will be taken away from those who reject Christ as the Capstone.

But who are the people who are referred to as not producing fruit? Some are the scribes and Pharisees who would never be saved as long as they persisted in their unbelief. Since the early church was predominantly Jewish, this passage cannot be interpreted as taking the kingdom of God away from Israel. It is also clear that the kingdom of God did not refer to the millennial kingdom. Taking all factors into consideration, what Jesus is saying is that those who reject the King will have the kingdom of God taken away from them and given to any people who produce its fruit—Jews and Gentiles. This is exactly what has happened in the church; both Jews and Gentiles who are saved become a part of the kingdom of God. In any case, it is clear that the Gentiles as a whole do not inherit the kingdom of God any more than unbelieving Israel does in the present age.

Another passage amillenarians use to try to justify the idea that Israel as a nation has been cast aside forever and its promises nullified is found in Romans 11:1–32, a passage already dealt with in part. However, as the opening verses of this chapter indicate, when Paul poses this question, "Did God reject his people?" his emphatic answer is, "By no means!" (Romans 11:1). As the chapter unfolds, the answer is that God has not rejected his people because he has a present purpose for them—becoming members of the body of Christ through faith in Christ—and a future for them when the present age is over and deliverance, the second coming of Christ, occurs.

On the basis of the evidence, Scripture supports the conclusion that Israel has a great future as a nation. The details of this future will be considered in later chapters.

The return of millions of Jews to the land of Israel in the twentieth century has focused the attention of the world on this tiny land. Does the Jew have any hope of ever having peace and tranquility in his ancient land? After all, does it belong to the Arab world or to Israel? Several wars and the extension of Israel to the west bank of Jordan have caused continual tension between Israel's claim on the land and Arab resistance to her expansion. From a theological point of view, the return of Jews to Israel has again raised the question of Israel's future. Many church scholars have held that Israel has no future as a nation, and for many years they predicted that Israel would never go back to her land.

The return of Jews to Israel has renewed the study of what the Bible promises Israel in regard to the future. Many have concluded that the Word of God promises Israel ultimate possession, and if she is already possessing a portion of her land, it raises the questions of whether the prophecies about the end of the present age are about to be fulfilled and whether the second coming of Christ may be near.

The Alignment of
Nations Suggests
His Coming

J. DWIGHT PENTECOST

J. Dwight Pentecost, Th.D.
Distinguished professor of Bible exposition
Dallas Theological Seminary
Author of more than twenty books

Until the time of the call of Abraham, God had been dealing with all men without any reference to their geographical or ethnic background. But with the call of Abraham, God made a division between Jew and Gentile. He said to Abraham in Genesis 12:3, "I will bless them that bless thee, and curse him that curseth thee: and in thee shall all families of the earth be blessed." In this promise God indicated that He had a program for Israel as a nation and also a program for Gentile nations, and that there would be blessing or cursing for both groups.

While the vast part of the Old Testament is concerned with the nation Israel, yet there also is a line of revelation concerning God's program for the Gentile nations. Such great themes as the revived Roman Empire, Armageddon, and the judgment on sheep and goats bring into focus the prophecies concerning the Gentiles. The specific program within these prophecies cannot be understood without some idea of God's division of nations.

The four areas into which the Gentile world powers will be divided at the time of the second advent of Christ will be considered, in order to see the significance in movements that are developing today. This cursory study of the fourfold division of Gentile nations will enable you to read your newspaper or news magazine more intelligently and understand some of the things that are taking place. Nations in the Word of God are divided on the basis of their relationship to the nation Israel, and it is impossible to study the prophetic program for the Gentiles without first seeing the relation of these Gentiles to Israel.

For the student of the prophetic scriptures, one of the most significant events in the last two thousand years was the event that took place in 1948 when the United Nations recognized Israel as a separate nation among the nations of the earth. It was significant because God's division of nations at the end times is a division on the basis of their geographical relation to the land of Israel or the land of Palestine. Nations at the end times will be divided into four different areas: north, south, east and west. Ezekiel 38 has the first division mentioned. This is the intriguing prophecy concerning God's judgment against Gog, the land of Magog (v. 2). Verse 15 says that Gog, who is the ruler, and Magog, the land over which he rules, "shalt come from thy place out of the north parts." On the basis of this verse, this man Gog from the land Magog is often referred to as the king of the north. He is called that because he will move against Palestine from his Homeland located North of Palestine.

On the basis of the nations mentioned in Genesis 10, Bible and prophetic students are generally agreed that the land of Magog is the land known today as Russia. Hebrew lexicons identify Magog as the land of Russia. The descendants of Noah following the flood separated to different points of the compass. The Japhethites left Mt. Ararat where the ark rested, which is in present-day Turkey, and traveled northward beyond the Caspian and Black seas and settled in that area known today as the southern part of Russia. Then those tribal people spread out from there, going northward, eastward, and westward, into what is now the central part of Europe. These people have continued from the time of Japheth in that area and will continue until the end times when, according to Ezekiel 38, Russia will bring about a movement of nations against the land of Palestine and will invade that land. While throughout all the Old Testament period, these people dwelled in the land, they lived there as an insignificant and unknown people. In New Testament times, even though that land was occupied by these Japhethites, they continued as an unknown people.

Down through history from the time of Christ to the present century, this densely populated area of the earth has been one that had little or no significance in international affairs. It was unknown, unrecognized, and consequently unfeared. And yet, the Word of God says that the final conflagration of nations will begin with an invasion of Palestine from the north. Prophecy anticipated the rise of a great nation, a great world power, from that area of the earth that had been totally unrecognized down through all the centuries of human history. When did Russia begin to emerge as a world power? Here is an amazing thing: a nation that at the beginning of this century was no more advanced physically, educationally, or scientifically than it was one thousand years ago has, within this century, come to the forefront among the nations of the earth. It was inconceivable a generation ago that they would ever dominate such a vast proportion of the earth's surface, and yet the Word of God says that at the end times the first great threat to the security of the nation Israel and the great threat to the world peace would not come from the Greeks or the Romans or the other highly educated, artistic people, but from a nation which would emerge out of the farthest north (Ezekiel 38:15). It was only a little over a generation ago that a few men introduced a system that has spread across the vast proportion of the earth's surface to become the most popular philosophy and ideology in the world today. Thus, the nation Israel has come into existence as a separate nation in your day and mine, and Russia, the king of the north, has risen to the place of world domination.

Daniel has a reference to a second great area into which the nations of the earth will be divided:

> And at the time of the end shall the king of the south push at him: and the king of the north shall come against him like a whirlwind (11:40).

The king of the north mentioned here is the same individual named in Ezekiel 38, but in Daniel a second alignment of nations is referred to as being under the "king of the south." This king of the south obviously must be the head of some nation that lies to the south of Palestine because that is the dividing point. Through the Old Testament the nation of Egypt was referred to as "the south" because for more that four hundred years Israel had been in bondage in Egypt. An Israelite in Moses' day knew that the land of the south was Egypt. Through the Old Testament, a reference to "the south" was a reference to Egypt. In Ezekiel 38:7, God said to the leader in Russia, or the king of the north, "Be thou a guard unto them," or as another version reads, "Be thou a commander unto them." This phrase shows that when Russia is ready to invade Palestine, she will have a number of allies under her control. One of these allies, according to Daniel 11:40, is referred to as the king of the south. Some of the other allies over which the king of the north is the commander are given in Ezekiel 38:5–6 as Persia, Ethiopia, Libya, Gomer, and Togarmah. There is no difficulty identifying Persia. But the names Ehiopia and Libya are used for two different areas in the Old Testament. On occasion they may refer to African Ethiopia and Libya, or they may refer to some of the area which today is called the Arab states, in the Arabian Peninsula, where Moses fled after he had killed the Egyptian. He married an Ethiopian, one of the daughters of that land. She was one of the Arab peoples, the descendants of Ishmael or Esau dwelling there. Evidently when he refers to Persia, Ethiopia, and Libya (v. 5), the prophet is referring to some of those Arab states who have come from Esau and Ismael, related to the Jews because of their descent from Abraham, but an unbelieving people. These will be referred to as the Arab states in the present study.

Along with these Arab states, Russia will be a commander to Gomer and Togarmah (v. 6). Gomer, according to Genesis 10, settled after the flood in the region of central Europe. Togarmah seems to refer to the land around the Caspian and Black seas, or the northern part of Turkey and the southern part of Russia. These names seem to suggest this second great group of nations that will be drawn together—Egypt together with the Arab states and Turkey and that section of the Middle East around the Caspian and Black seas. For general reference, this will be called the Pan-Arab block in this study; it is referred to as moving under the authority of the king of the south.

How long ago in history did Egypt rise out of the dust of

nations to take a significant place in world affairs? It has been within our generation. With the rise of Nasser, Egypt emerged out of the darkness that had gripped it. Out of an insignificant place among the nations, she has come to dominate the Middle East. Thus this group of nations has come together under the authority of Egypt, the one called the king of the south in Daniel 11.

But this passage tells another significant thing: the king of the south is not independent and does not act on his own authority. He moves when the king of the north tells him to. What does it mean? If we understand these prophecies aright, it means that the Pan-Arab block will be controlled by Russia and will move only when Russia tells them to do so. All of this took place not hundreds of years ago but in our generation. Perhaps God is trying to tell us something; for He not only has brought Russia to a place of prominence, but He also is aligning the Arab states under the leadership of Egypt, and Egypt is bringing them over under the leadership of Russia—and all of this is taking place simultaneously.

In Revelation 16:12 is a reference to a third division:

The sixth angel poured out his vial upon the great river Euphrates: and the water thereof was dried up, that the way of the kings of the east might be prepared.

The king of the east. There is scant reference in the Word of God to this division of world power, but several significant facts are pointed out here. The kings of the east come from lands that are east of the Euphrates River, which was the known world's boundary in Old Testament days. But the prophet speaks of an invasion of Palestine when the kings that will come from beyond the Euphrates will move against the Middle East and catapult the world into yet another conflagration at the end of the tribulation period. Who are these kings of the east? They cannot be identified as can the states in Ezekiel 38 because specific names are not mentioned.

But one very significant movement is taking place today. China has declared herself as independent from Russia. From the time of Russian domination of China, Russia looked at China as a part of her sphere of influence. The ideology of Russia was superimposed on China, and yet, wonder of wonders, a nation—one about which we know almost nothing today because it is entirely behind the Bamboo Curtain—has revolted against Russia, has declared itself independent of their authority and has launched out on a militancy that even goes beyond the militancy of Red Russia. This division between Russia and China was necessary, Bible students have felt, but they took it by faith. If the kings of the east are to invade Palestine separate from the king of the north, there had to be some division. But not today. For now this rupture is so complete that nations are coming to be so afraid of China that they are looking with kindness even upon Russia. The kings of the east seem to be forming.

The fourth sphere is a coalition of powers that might be referred to as the kings of the west, although Scripture does not call them that. Daniel said four world powers would rule Israel: Babylon, Medo-Persia, Greece, and Rome (chaps 2, 7). He further stated that the Roman Empire in its historical development would fall into division and out of the old Roman Empire there would emerge ten separate nations. This is inferred in the vision of the image with the ten toes or the beast with the ten horns. Those ten toes and ten horns represented the nations that emerged out of

the old Roman Empire. Some of those nations are Italy and
France, the Low Countries, Spain and Britain. When the Roman
Empire dissolved, the power that was once centralized in Rome
divided itself out among these emerging member nations, and
they have continued in that separate state and will do so until the
tribulation period, that brief period just before the Lord's return to
this earth in glory. Then those nations will come together and elect
one man to become head over them, as described in Revelation
17:13.

What has been the history of Europe since World War II? Plan
after plan, program after program has been designed to do basically one thing—bring Europe together into a united states of
Europe. First there were the military alliances, such as NATO, that
tied them together. Then there was the Common Market movement that tied them together economically. And within these
movements there has been a progression of political union that
will eventually see the nations of Europe federating together to
form a United States of Europe as the original colonies in this
country formed the United States of America. This is a post-World
War II development. This is of great significance. The problem in
Europe today is the problem of cooperation between these nations
that have emerged out of the old Roman Empire and have gone
their independent ways for centuries, but now are exploring the
ways and means by which they might come together under one
head.

Thus, this is the fourth area of political power that is developing in the very direction that prophecy said Gentile nations
would move just before Christ's second advent. The king of the
north has arisen to try to take over the control of the world. The
second great prophesied division, the king of the south has come

into existence, and these fiercely independent peoples have come together in an alliance, the Pan-Arab block, under the leadership of Egypt and are making overtures to Russia to join with them. At the same time, the third great area has come into existence so that a separate power exists in the Orient, the kings of the east. In addition, movements in Europe toward federation are discussed in every newspaper and news magazine. All of these programs will come to their fulfillment after the church is translated and believers have been caught up and received unto glory. They will come to their fulfillment in the tribulation period.

But if in our day we can see the hand of God moving toward the completion of those programs that will be fulfilled in the tribulation, and if the rapture has to take place before the fulfillment of these, who can say that the rapture could not take place right now? One would have to be spiritually blind or grossly ignorant to miss the fact that the hand of God is moving nations, raising up nations that historians said would never rise again, and bringing about alliances of nations and divisions among nations that historians and political scientists have said could never be accomplished. In the last twenty years more has happened in international affairs than has happened for two thousand years, and it has happened according to God's guidebook. God knew what He would do when He foretold what would take place at the end times. Thus God's Word gives the child of God assurance and comfort, and kindles his hope that the time of Christ's coming draws nigh.

THE KINGS OF THE EAST

Events taking place in the Orient today seem to give one more indication that God is preparing the stage and putting all the actors in place for the final world drama, and is waiting to raise the curtain by the rapture of the church so that these events can take place. To understand the significance of "the kings of the east" or the Oriental powers in prophecy, remember that during the latter days—that brief period between the rapture of the church and the second advent of Christ which is called the tribulation period—the world will be divided into four different political spheres of influence. The first will be under the king of the south, that is, Egypt and the Arab states. The second sphere will be that of the king of the north, or Russia. According to Ezekiel 38, these two spheres are allied together. Russia is spoken of as a commander over the other peoples and nations, and it seems from this passage of Scripture that the Arab states will draw closer and closer to Russia until they are completely under her influence and following her bidding.

The great final world conflagration referred to in Scripture as the campaign of Armageddon will begin in the middle of the tribulation period, that is, three and a half years after the translation of the church into glory, but three and a half years before the second advent of Jesus Christ back to the earth. At that time Russia will suggest to the Arab states that they move into Palestine and capture it. They will urge the Arab states to make this move with the promise that when they move in from the south, Russia simultaneously will move in from the north. They will converge on Jerusalem and overrun the land. This invasion is described in detail in Ezekiel 38. Then Ezekiel 39 says that when these two political powers meet together in Jerusalem to destroy the land and occupy it, God will destroy that political sphere of influence. Those two federations of nations will be destroyed the same way as Sodom and Gomorrah were destroyed in the book of Genesis.

One can readily realize in our present world situation that if Russia and all her allies were suddenly and catastrophically destroyed, a vacuum would result. Evidently when God destroys these two allies (Russia and the Arab states), the western confederacy (the United States of Europe) will take advantage of the vacuum and move in to occupy the land of Palestine. According to Daniel 11:45, after Russia is removed as a sphere of influence, the head of the European confederacy will move into the region of Jerusalem and set up his headquarters there. Revelation 13:7 says that "the beast," that is, the head of the United States of Europe, will make war with the saints and overcome them.

Notice the next word in verse 7: "Power was given him over all kindreds, and tongues, and nations." This is part of the satanic program of deception, because God from the early chapters of the Old Testament has decreed that He is going to make Jesus Christ the King. Jesus Christ is destined to be King of kings and Lord of lords, and all authority will be given to Him. But Satan will put an imitator on the throne, and Satan's puppet, this one called "the little horn" in Daniel or "the beast" in Revelation, or the "abomination that desolates" in Matthew 24 will become the head of the United States of Europe. As such he will claim worldwide authority. How will it be possible for him to do that in light of the fact that there will be another great sphere of political influence in the latter days, the sphere called in Revelation 16:12 "the kings of the east"? First, it is of great significance that in the days in which we live there should have been a division between Russian Communism and Chinese Communism. According to Ezekiel 38, when God destroys Russia in the middle of the tribulation period, not only will Russia be destroyed and her power broken, but the power of all her allies will be broken as well. Since that is true, if China and the Orient were allied with Russia at the time of the destruction of Russia, the Oriental powers would be wiped out, and it would be impossible for them to revive and become a great antagonist against the authority of this world dictator who is coming.

Although we Bible teachers, in the light of that prophetic picture, expected a break between Russian Communism and Chinese Communism, we were somewhat surprised that it took place before the rapture. Many assumed they would remain as allies until we were in glory, and then that rift would take place. But this rift between the two nations is becoming wider and wider today, until students of international affairs feel there is an irreconcilable gulf between the two.

Another thing to observe is that throughout the Word of God, until Revelation, no reference is made to the Oriental peoples. They had no influence nor effect on Israel in the Old Testament, and no reference was made of them in the New Testament. The missionary journeys that covered the world covered the Roman world, but not the Oriental world, according to the Word of God. Not until the book of Revelation is any mention made of these kings of the east. As far as the biblical world was concerned, the Tigris and Euphrates rivers were the easternmost boundary, and no reference is made to what was beyond the Euphrates River. Yet, those peoples were there, and in God's own time they would have a significant part to play. But the first real reference to them is in Revelation 9 and they are referred to again in chapter 16. Revelation 9 reveals an interesting fact. The apostle John has been describing the great judgments that God will pour out upon the earth during the tribulation. The first series of judgments that will be poured out is described as the breaking of seals, and then there is a second series of judgment pictured as the blowing of trumpets. In 9:13, the sixth angel is blowing on the sixth trumpet. He is describing one of the judgments that God will pour out upon the earth as an evidence of divine wrath. In verse 14, the sixth angel which had the trumpets said, "Loose the four angels which are bound in the great river Euphrates."

Throughout the book of Revelation, angels are used by God as restrainers. They hold things in check so that a program cannot get ahead of its time. God is working according to the strictest timetable and, so that Satan cannot interfere, He has given certain angels the responsibility of thwarting Satan's program and keeping it in check, and not until God permits the restraining angels to remove the restraint can Satan's program develop. Revelation 9:14 says a restraint has been exercised that kept certain peoples or armies beyond the Euphrates River so they couldn't cross it. Scripture does not particularly identify these peoples beyond the great river Euphrates. It simply says they are peoples that come from beyond the Euphrates River, and no further attempt is made to describe them. Therefore, it is impossible to identify them as any specific people to the exclusion of all others, but perhaps this may be a coalition of nations since they are called "kings." They may be identified as Asiatic or Oriental peoples and could include such nations as India, Pakistan, China, and Japan, who have been kept out of the sphere of influence that God has given to Israel. God has kept them beyond the Tigris and Euphrates rivers. Verse 15 says, "And the four angels were loosed, which were prepared for an hour, and a day, and a month, and a year, for to slay the third part of men."

God says He will pour a judgment on the earth that will remove one-third of the earth's population from off the earth. This judgment, of such magnitude that it staggers the imagination, is in the form of a marching army. "The number of the army of the horsemen were two hundred thousand thousand, and I heard the number of them." Two hundred thousand thousand is two hundred million. This army is ready to move and bring death and destruction in its wake which will remove one-third of the men. Then, in very figurative language in verses 18–19, the army is described. Since in John's day they didn't have tanks or armored weapons, the most formidable weapon an army could use was an armored horse. John is describing this future army in terms of the most awesome and dreaded piece of military equipment that existed in his day. That is why he describes them as horses prepared for battle. They have breastplates, making them invincible. Their heads are like lions; that is, they can destroy as a lion destroys its prey. "Out of their mouths issued fire and smoke and brimstone." They brought destruction in their wake. One of the most dreaded pieces of military equipment was burning pitch or burning sulfur; and this army brings that kind of destruction. Verse 19 says,

> For their power is in their mouth, and in their tails: for their tails were like unto serpents, and had heads, and with them they do hurt.

He describes the army as a poisonous serpent which can bring death in its wake. This is a very graphic picture of the awesome destruction that this advancing army will spread.

Consider this problem: Beyond the Euphrates is an empire so great, a political sphere of influence so powerful, that it can mass an army of 200 million men. In the light of this existence of this power, how can the head of the United State of Europe claim worldwide power and authority? The problem is, how can this man move his capital to Jerusalem and say, "I am the emperor of the whole world" while there is a sphere of influence strong enough to mass an army of 200 million men? Now either this man trying to rule the world from Jerusalem is a complete idiot or something has happened that to all intents and purposes has nullified the power of this great Oriental confederacy. It may be that this army composed of 200 million men is so occupied with internal affairs instead of external affairs that it can give no attention to anything taking place outside of its own boundary.

Some time ago a student rushed into my office and said, "Do you have a radio?" I said, "No." And he said, "You didn't hear the broadcast, then?" I said, "No." He was just trembling with excitement. He said, "I heard a broadcast that was relayed by way of Japan from Red China that the Chinese leader had threatened the rebels in his nation with extermination, saying that at his word he could assemble an army of 200 million men to put down the riots." That student had read Revelation 9 before, and no wonder he was so excited.

It seems reasonable to suggest that this large group of men to be slain will not be killed through the march of this army outside of the Orient beyond the Euphrates, but they will be destroyed as this army seeks to put down the revolt and riots within the nations beyond the Euphrates River. They will be so occupied with internal affairs that the head of the United States of Europe, who will set himself up as the world dictator, will feel that the Oriental nations are in such chaos he doesn't have to take them into consideration. After all, Washington operates on just such a basis in dealing with Red China today.

It seems as though John is suggesting in Revelation 9 that one of the great judgments that God will pour out upon the earth will be in the territory of the kings of the east, and that in order to suppress the revolutions and the rebellions against that autocratic power, a third of the earth's population will be destroyed. More than a third of the earth's population exists within the confines of the Oriental nations today, and that 200 million men could conceivably be brought to bear to try to consolidate authority in these Oriental nations and, in consolidating authority, death will be on such a wide scale that the third part of men shall be destroyed. On the basis of what seems to be inferred in this chapter of the Revelation, great significance can be given to the present revolution going on within Communist China, and it is interesting to see the struggle for power there and to follow the steps that the leaders are taking to keep control within the nation. This would answer the question as to how this head of the United States of Europe could proclaim himself a world dictator, and how he could exert authority over the earth without ever being challenged by the Oriental nations who could mass such a great military movement.

Revelation 16 has another brief and yet significant word about the kings of the east. God will pour out a third series of judgments on the earth, and these judgments are symbolized by the emptying of bowls or vials. In the sixth vial, which is the next to the last judgment that God will pour out upon the earth, John says,

> And the sixth angel poured out his vial upon the great river Euphrates; and the water thereof was dried up, that the way of the kings of the east might be prepared (16:12).

This brings us to the very end of the tribulation period. Russia and the Arab states will have been out of the picture for approximately three and a half years. Jerusalem has become the capital of the empire ruled over by the head of the United States of Europe, who has proclaimed himself as both king and god on his throne, and has demanded that all the world worship him. He has instituted such a regimented system that no man can buy or sell unless he has that identifying mark of submission to the beast. But after he rules for three and a half years and is revered by a godless world as their god, God will step in and show the world that this demon-possessed man is not God. All this time the angels will have been keeping the Oriental nations in the Orient. God will suddenly take away that restraint—pictured in Revelation 16:12 as the waters of the Euphrates drying up. When God dried up the Red Sea, the Israelites could leave Egypt on dry land. Forty years later when God dried up the Jordan, the Israelites who had been in the wilderness could march into the land. The drying up of the waters then provided a way of access. God will dry up the Euphrates, that is, provide a way of access so that the Oriental powers that could mass an army of 200 million to try to suppress revolt within the nation will be able to spill over and begin a march across the fertile crescent toward Palestine. They will come because of their determination to challenge the right of the head of the federated states of Europe who claims worldwide dominion. These two political spheres will prepare for battle, gathering together "into a place called in the Hebrew tongue Armageddon" (v. 16).

Armageddon is the great plain of Esdralon in the north of Palestine that stretches from Mount Carmel forty miles across to the Sea of Galilee. Napoleon marched across it, declaring that it was the world's greatest natural battlefield. It is that battlefield to which God will bring together the armies of the United States of

Europe and the armies of the Orient who will be preparing to enter into battle to see who will rule the world. At that time a most significant thing will take place.

> After the tribulation of those days shall the sun be darkened, and the moon shall not give her light, and the stars shall fall from heaven, and the powers of the heavens shall be shaken (Matthew 24:29).

Now, notice: "And then shall appear the sign of the Son of man in heaven"(v. 30).

The sign that God was present in Israel was the pillar of fire or cloud that reflected God's glory. Israel knew that God was in the tabernacle because of the shining of the glory of God. The day will come when this world will see the shining of the glory of God again when the sign of the Son of man appears in the heaven. As a light that outshines the brightness of the sun, God's glory will be revealed, and men shall see the sign of the Son of man in the clouds of heaven. What will be their response? When Israel saw the glory of God manifested in their camp, they fell and worshipped; and when the glory of God moved, they followed. But in Revelation 19:19, John says,

> And I saw the beast, and the kings of the earth, and their armies that would include both the kings of the east as well as the western confederacy gathered together to make war against him that sat on the horse, and against his army.

When these two military powers are coming to do battle to settle the question as to who will rule the world, suddenly the light of the glory of God will appear in the heavens, and they will recognize this as an invasion—if you please—from outer space. They will recognize that this is God moving in to judge, and those two nations that were ready to battle each other will suddenly join together to fight against the Lord Jesus Christ, the one described in Revelation 19:11–16 as the victorious Commander on the white horse whose name is the King of kings and the Lord of lords. These two groups will never get to use their weapons on each other; they never will fire a shot. The issue as to which one of them will rule the world will never be settled, because the Lord Jesus Christ will come to this earth and, according to Revelation 11:15, "The kingdoms of this world are become the kingdoms of our Lord, and of his Christ; and he shall reign for ever and ever."

This will be the greatest display of military might that the world has ever seen, and if 200 million men can be raised up to control affairs within the Oriental nations, think of how many they would send out when they embark on world conquest. Think of the unnumbered multitudes who will gather together under the authority of the commander of the west. But those nations, even though they join together against the Lord Jesus Christ, will not be able to prevent His return, nor will they be able to thwart His judgment, for a sword shall go out of His mouth and He shall destroy those multiplied millions in a moment of time in order that He might be King of kings and Lord of lords.

In the light of the fact that the final battle of this world's history is to be between the east and the west, it is of great significance that within the last decade the east has broken off completely from the west—China has completely broken with Russia. It is also significant that China will be going through such a time of turmoil that her leaders will have to spend their effort and energy to consolidate their authority within their empire. When God removes restraints and they march to battle they will be going out to meet the one who is the Judge of all men. He will put down all rebellion, destroy all military might, and rule as King of kings and Lord of lords. In the light of these references in the Bible, a whole new dimension is added to the reading of newspapers and magazines as we watch the developments in the east, for God is restraining the kings of the east until He will draw the east and the west into battle. Then Jesus Christ shall put down the mightiest gathering of military men the world has known so that He might demonstrate how great are the authority and the power that belong to His Son.

The Condition of the
Church Indicates
His Coming

DAVID JEREMIAH

David Jeremiah, D. D.
Senior pastor, Shadow Mountain Community Church
Host, Turning Point, a national radio ministry
Author of numerous books

Some people don't think churches are important. "I have my private way of worshiping—don't need four walls and a preacher," they say.

God thinks churches are important and when He gave John the vision, it was almost as if He were looking through a magnifying glass at our churches today.

The world is full of churches; in almost every one of our American towns there's a white church with a steeple, a stone church covered with vines, a modern church built at angles, and usually the church with the most impressive stained-glass windows.

Some churches have chairs down the aisles and people standing in the foyer; in others the pastor stares over empty rows to reach the eyes of the timid souls in the back.

God is not a member of one denomination or another. When

Jesus was teaching His disciples He asked them, "'Who do you say I am?' Peter answered, 'You are the Christ, the Son of the living God.' Jesus replied, 'Blessed are you, Simon son of Jonah, for this was not revealed to you by man, but by my Father in heaven. And I tell you that you are Peter, and on this rock I will build my church, and the gates of Hades will not overcome it'" (Matthew 16:15–18).

The Rock upon which the church is built is not Peter. The Rock is Christ Himself, as Paul clearly said, "...and that rock was Christ" (1 Corinthians 10:4).

The only true church is made up of individuals who have accepted Jesus Christ as Savior. Within every church building or denominational structure there are true members of the church and there are others who call themselves church members simply because they are in the directory.

Jesus wrote seven letters to seven literal churches in Asia Minor during the first century. However, these letters have not been assigned to the national archives to gather dust. They are as current as today's calendar, and they offer a chronological account of church history.

These churches were real; people attended services in them and listened to the messages. Although the letters were written in the first century, they apply to our contemporary churches and have personal value to every believer. The letters begin with the first century church and end with the last type of church which will be on earth at the end of the age.

Church Shopping

How do we choose a church home? Many churches believe they must have a dynamic, young, good-looking pastor with a wife who raises three beautiful children, plays the piano, and conducts a weekly Bible class. Other churches think they will attract the masses with a lavish sanctuary, a magnificent pipe organ, or a well-equipped kitchen. However, none of these influence a church's growth or decline as significantly as how much love and acceptance people experience when they attend.

The Institute for American Church Growth in Pasadena (California) conducted a survey of 8,600 people from congregations in thirty-nine denominations to measure their "love-care" quotient. Here's what they learned: members of growing churches are more loving to each other and to visitors. Loving churches, regardless of their theology, denomination, or location—attract more people.

The first church of Ephesus had some serious love problems, just as some modern churches do.

Letter to Ephesus: The Evangelical Church

Ephesus was one of the urban centers in the Roman empire. It was a cosmopolitan city of rich and poor, cultured and ignorant, a gathering place for false religious cults and superstitions. The temple of Diana, one of the seven wonders of the world, was there. This shrine served as the bank of Asia, an art gallery, and a sanctuary for criminals; the city derived much of its wealth from the manufacture and sale of images of the goddess.

The letter began on a positive note:

"I know your deeds, your hard work and your perseverance. I know that you cannot tolerate wicked men, that you have tested those who claim to be apostles but are not, and found them false. You have persevered and have endured hardships for my name, and have not grown weary" (Revelation 2:2, 3).

When Paul made Ephesus a center for evangelism during the three years he spent there, the church apparently flourished. After Paul's release from prison, he probably visited the city again and established Timothy as the pastor. John may have succeeded Timothy. A fairly impressive group of ministers, wouldn't you say?

The Ephesian congregation was dynamic and its annual report must have looked good. It would never have matched this report I saw recently: "Annual report...New members: none. Baptisms: none. Gifts to missions: none." Then at the bottom of the report the church clerk had written, "Brethren, pray for us that we might be faithful unto the end."

The Ephesian church persevered through times of trouble. One of my heroes in the faith is Charles Spurgeon. He said: "Pray God to send a few men with what the Americans call 'grit' in them; men, who when they know a thing to be right, will not turn away, or turn aside, or stop; men who will persevere all the more because there are difficulties to meet or foes to encounter."[1]

Church discipline was prevalent in the Ephesian church. If someone falsely claimed to be an apostle, he was called a liar. Today there are churches where the leaders claim to be apostles. The Ephesians would not have accepted those men; they were careful to examine visiting ministers to see if they were genuine.

They also despised the Nicolaitans, a sect which led a life of self-indulgence and immorality. A true love for God involves a fervent aversion to those who counterfeit and distort the purity of biblical truth.

Sounds like a great church, doesn't it? It was dynamic, dedicated, patient, disciplined, and discerning. But Jesus saw past all the pious facade; the church of Ephesus had heart trouble!

"Yet I hold this against you: You have forsaken your first love" (Revelation3:4).

What a shock to be told that you don't love Christ as you once did. Love should grow, not wither. One commentator wrote: "To have something against friend or brother may be very human…But when it is the Lord who has something against the church, it is time to tremble; and when that thing is loss of love, the church should fall on its knees."[2]

These Ephesians (and the spiritual Ephesians of our time) had stopped loving Christ and each other the way they once had done.

We hear the same about marriage. "I just don't love him any more," the wife complains to a counselor. What happened to the girl whose heart beat faster when she heard his car outside? Where is the man who used to bring flowers and tell her how lucky he was to have found her? The "Ephesian" marriages have lost the thrill of first love.

Once the diagnosis has been made, the prescription can be written. Here are three steps to renewing love:

First, *remember* what it was like. Relive the thrill of romance, the desire to tell the world of its wonder. When I see the tears of joy in the eyes of men, women, and children who have accepted Jesus as Savior, when I perform a marriage and see the transformation on the faces of that couple as they look at each other, I want to touch them and say, "Beloved, don't lose your first love."

Second, *repent* and turn your life around. Make a conscious vow to make that relationship right again.

Third, *repeat*—"do the things you did at first"—those acts of love, even if you don't feel like it. Do it and the feelings will follow.

Talk about revival in the church, or in a marriage! It can explode!

Jesus warned the church at Ephesus that it would lose its light and its testimony in the community, if the first love was not revived (Revelation 2:5). This actually happened many years later when Ephesus declined as a city. It is now uninhabited and one of the major ruins of the area.

What a warning this is to churches that have lost their first love. When my wife and I were in Europe we visited beautiful churches with graveyard interiors. We went to the great tabernacle in London where Charles Spurgeon once preached to overflow audiences. My heart was saddened to sit in that vast worship hall with less than a hundred people in attendance.

Surrounding us in every country are church buildings which are no more than clerical caskets, lined in rich satin, gilded with gold, and buried in complacency.

Looking at the outside, the church at Ephesus appeared to be a model church. However, inside the love was growing cold, the people were involved in their "good works" out of a sense of duty. The historical era of this church was A.D. 33–100.

Christ ends every one of His letters to the churches with the same conclusion: "He who has an ear, let him hear what the Spirit says to the churches" (Revelation 2:7).

Are we able to hear the warning signs that we are losing our first love? Where is the excitement we experienced as new believers in Jesus Christ? Where is the thrill of looking at the wife or husband we adored when we were first married? *Love is abused when it is not used.*

In our busy lives we may allow our love relationship with the Lord to grow weak. The church at Ephesus has an important message for us: the Lord is to have priority in our lives. Personally, I could stop at the first letter and have my heart burn with conviction. I know there are times when I slip into Ephesus, and I do not like the atmosphere.

Letter to Smyrna: The Iron Curtain Church

Corrie ten Boom recalled a childhood incident when she told her father, "I am afraid that I will never be strong enough to die as a martyr."

He said, "When you have to go on a journey, when do I give you the money for the fair—two weeks before?"

"No, Daddy, on the day that I am leaving."

"Precisely…and our wise Father in heaven knows when we're going to need things, too. When the time comes to die, you will find the strength you need—just in time."

In later years, Corrie was imprisoned in Ravensbruk, the infamous German prison camp where more than 50,000 women were killed. She wrote, "It is necessary, when we prepare ourselves for the end-time, also to be prepared to die for Jesus."[3]

Living in a country where we are not tortured or killed for our faith in Jesus, it seems remote that we might be called upon to be martyrs. However, martyrdom is not just a torturing death. What if we lose our jobs because we're Christians? What if our children are taunted because they believe in Jesus Christ? Suffering takes many forms.

The letter to the church at Smyrna was personally written to people under pressure. Every word He speaks to this suffering body is one of appreciation. Only two of the seven churches received letters of total commendation and encouragement: Smyrna is one and Philadelphia is the other.

Smyrna was the proudest and most beautiful city of Asia. It is considered by historians as the most exquisite city the Greeks ever built. The city sloped to the sea, and along the sides of the hill was a large amphitheater, where over 20,000 people could sit. It was there that the worship of Caesar was centered.

By the time the book of Revelation was written, emperor worship was compulsory. The churches were persecuted because they wouldn't bow down to Caesar and burn incense in the temple dedicated to *Kaiser Kurios,* Caesar is Lord!

The Christians who refused to obey the emperor's decree were marked men, traitors against the government. To be a Christian in the Roman Empire during that bloody era was to live in jeopardy every day; the tortures inflicted on these men of faith were despicable. Some Christians were strapped on the rack (a wheel about two feet wide and eight feet tall), their ankles chained to the floor and wrists tied to the wheel. Every time the believer was asked to deny the Lord and refused, the rack was tightened until he was ripped limb for limb. Other Christians were thrown into boiling oil, or mangled by hungry lions in the coliseum.

The church at Smyrna was pulled apart by pressure, poverty, and persecution. Most of us cannot comprehend what it would be like to have our fingernails torn out or to see our children slaughtered before our eyes. Jesus gave two commands to this suffering family. He told them to be fearless, just as David wrote in those famous words, "Even thought I walk through the valley of the shadow of death, I will fear no evil" (Psalm 23).

He told the believers in Smyrna to be faithful, even to the point of death. Are we, at the human level, capable of such sacrifice?

The Church in Today's Catacombs is a book that documents the stories of people who suffered under the brutality of the communist regime, or had been eyewitnesses to the suffering of others. The brutal acts performed on these martyrs were so inhuman we could not repeat the obscenities our Christian brothers and sisters endured behind the Iron Curtain.

Suzanne Labin wrote: "...Romans, Mongolians, and Hitlerites did not torture their own followers. Communism has set this last precedent. It has killed with the worst sufferings ten thousand times as many Communists as have all the anti-Communist regimes put together. Even wolves do not devour each other. But Communists do. It is a madman's world."[4]

The Christians at Smyrna lived in a world where they were despised for their faith. Christ encouraged them by telling them that through every trial they would ever have, He understood. The one who was slandered, falsely accused, whipped, brutally beaten, and hung upon a Roman cross said, "I know your afflictions and your poverty—yet you are rich!" (Revelation 2:9).

He knew persecution and poverty, and yet He reminded His followers that they were rich! The Lord's values are different from those of the world.

He said, "you will suffer persecution for ten days" (Revelation 2:10). I believe the intent of His words was to prepare the church for the suffering that would be brief in contrast to eternity.

The pastor of the church in Smyrna was a student and disciple of John. His name was Polycarp, and he was the messenger (angel) of whom Christ spoke when John wrote this second letter. Polycarp's ministry ended in A.D. 156 when persecution of Christians increased and they were tortured and thrown to the wild beasts. Polycarp was marched into the amphitheater where a mob was waiting to see what form of ghoulish pleasure they could get from his violent death. As he stood before the proconsul, he was commanded to deny Christ, but he replied, "Eighty-six years have I served Him and He never did me any harm; how then can I blaspheme my King and my Savior?"

As the old man stood before the crowd in the stadium, the governor shouted, "I'll have you destroyed by fire, unless you change your attitude."

Polycarp answered: "You threaten me with fire which burns for an hour and after a little is extinguished. But you are ignorant of the fires of the coming judgment and of eternal punishment reserved for the ungodly. But why do you delay? Bring on what you will."

The crowd gathered wood and threw torches on the pyre. Their hatred was bitter and they cheered as the godly man was brought to the stake. As the flames began to curl around his body, Polycarp prayed:

"I thank you that you have graciously thought me worthy of this day and of this hour, that I may be a part of the number of martyrs to die for Christ."[5]

Perhaps we have become so refined in our teaching of Bible truths that we are softening the shouts of the martyrs. Christians throughout time have been persecuted for their faith. Some of us today may be called upon to suffer in our own lifetimes.

Letter to Pergamum: The Inner City Church

Times Square in New York City spills the putrid breath of its porno shops, X-rated movies, prostitutes, and drug dealers into neon-lit streets. Enticements can beckon in subtle ways with promises of easy love and cheap thrills. Every town, school, and business houses the potential of Satan's city.

If we had entered Pergamum, the capitol of Asia, we might have been caught breathless by its beauty. It was built on a rocky hill, where the Mediterranean could be seen on a clear day (it probably wasn't plagued by smog). Pergamum was a cultural center, famous for its library that was said to house 200,000 rolls of parchment. I imagine the city attracted the finest minds in the academic world. However, Jesus didn't write to the professors in their ivory towers, but to Christians, struggling to keep their faith amidst the critics of higher learning. He called Pergamum "Satan's city," which may not have pleased the professors and bibliophiles.

The city was deeply entrenched in the worship of the god of healing, and the temples of Asclepius where like the hospitals in the ancient world. The emblem of Asclepius was the coiled snake that appeared on many of the coins of the city. Today, the coiled snake on a staff is the insignia of the medical profession. Perhaps our doctors might not want to know that the symbol originated in Satan's city!

The believers in that city may have been like Christians today who sit in classrooms and listen to learned teachers scoff at Christian beliefs or undercut their values. They were commended because "...you remain true to my name. You did not renounce your faith in me, even in the days of Antipas, my faithful witness..." (Revelation 2:12). (Antipas was slowly roasted to death in a bronze kettle.)

However, Christ said, "Nevertheless, I have a few things against you" (Revelation 2:14). The Pergamum believers may have looked at each other and said, "What have we done?" They had become compromisers. Satan did not make a frontal attack by coming in as a roaring lion (1 Peter 5:8). He slithered in the back door and led them astray as a deceiving serpent.

Jesus told them there were certain members of the Pergamum congregation who were following weird teaching. Some were listening to doctrines of Balaam, and others to the Nicolaitans (Revelation 2:14, 15).

In each of the churches so far, Satan has had a different strategy. The Ephesian church had lost its first love. In Smyrna, the cruelty of Satan came from outside forces. In Pergamum, Satan used the approach Balaam used against Israel.

Balaam was a prophet who said he could influence the gods for or against men by his incantations and offerings. He ran a wholesale business in divine favors, so Balak, king of Moab, offered Balaam a nice profit if he could bring down a curse on the king's despised enemies in Israel.

Balaam tried to command God, but instead of a curse, Israel was blessed. Balaam's plan backfired. Frustrated by his failure to get what he wanted, he showed Balak how he could corrupt Israel by having the adulterous Mabite women seduce the Israelite men. This plan worked, and Balaam was the prime mover in the fall of Israel. His tactic was, "If you can't curse them, corrupt them" (Numbers 22–25).

The sin of Pergamum, just as that of Balaam, was the toleration of evil. Worldly standards had crept into their fellowship. Today it's the same worldly spirit within the church which makes it difficult to distinguish between the actions of Christians and the lifestyles of non-Christians. When those who call themselves Christians commit adultery, cheat in business, or lower their moral standards to suit the situation, they fit into the Pergamum mentality.

The compromising Christians in Pergamum heard the same command that is heard today: "Repent therefore!"

God gives His rewards for turning our lives from compromise

to commitment. He loves us enough to forgive us, but He will not force that love upon us.

After the call for repentance, there are two promises from the Lord: "I will give some of the hidden manna. I will also give him a white stone with a new name written on it, known only to him who receives it" (Revelation 2:17).

"Hidden manna" from heaven is the nourishment needed for spiritual health. I remember as a seminary student in Dallas, I worked in a freight yard. The job was hard physical labor and my working companions used pretty raw language and jokes. One day, during our lunch break, I noticed a new fellow hunched in a corner with his "hidden manna," a well-worn New Testament. He chose not to compromise, no matter what surrounded him.

In ancient courts, white and black stones signified the verdicts of juries. A black stone meant guilty; a white stone meant acquittal. The Christian is acquitted in the sight of God because of the work of Jesus Christ. The verdict is not guilty.

Modern counterparts to members of the church in Pergamum have muddied their Christian commitment with compromise. So much of the world is in the church and so many of the church are in the world that there is no difference between the two.

The Pergamum period of history evolved into an era when Christianity was introduced by force.

The "Christian Emperor"

Ephesus represents the period of the apostles; Smyrna represents the period of persecution during the second and third centuries. When Diocletian, the last persecuting emperor of that era, failed to stamp out the church, Constantine came into power. Tradition has it that Constantine looked up and saw a vision in the shape of a cross which said, *in hoc signo vinces:* "By this sign conquer." That night, Constantine bargained with Satan to join the church and declare himself a Christian. Christianity, said Emperor Constantine, was to be the religion of the state.

Christian leaders were invited to watch the wholesale baptism of entire regiments of soldiers in Constantine's army. Christianity was forced on unwilling subjects at sword point: baptism or death! The unholy alliance of church and state resulted.

In the early part of the third century, the Pergamum church was married to the world. True believers, who had been previously persecuted, were now lauded by political and civil authorities. Constantine assumed leadership of the church; pagan temples became Christian churches; heathen festivals were converted into Christian ones. Idols were named after so-called Christian saints. Many Christians who had suffered were now welcomed to the imperial palace and they swallowed the bait, sacrificing allegiance to Christ, and becoming locked in fatal union with compromise. Constantine was now called Pontifex Maximus and assumed leadership of the church.

Out of this alliance between the Roman emperor and the Christian church came the birth of Roman Catholocism.

Letter to Thyatira: The Suburban Church

The next church to receive an important letter was in Thyatira, a place quite the opposite of Ephesus. Instead of shriveled love, it had growing love; the people worked hard, faithfully, and patiently. Beneath the healthy surface, however, was a cesspool.

A modern man, cut in the mold of the Thyatiran church, received a memo on his desk, requesting his appearance at two o'clock in the boss's office. At 1:59 he walked in, wiping his sweaty palms on his sides. After a pleasant greeting, the boss said, "Sit down, I want to tell you some positive things I've observed about your work." The fellow eased himself into the chair in front of the executive desk and the knot in his stomach began to dissolve. Maybe he'd get a raise.

"You're a good worker, and you seem to believe strongly in what you're doing."

A grin crossed his face as he tried to be humble about his achievements. All the overtime hadn't been in vain.

"Nevertheless," the boss continued, "I have evidence that you are frequently seen with a woman who is not your wife."

The man behind the desk seemed to have eyes that could look right through the accused employee. Adultery may not be an indictment in many companies, but in this case the worker was the youth pastor in a large church.

When Jesus wrote the letter to the pastor of the church in Thyatira He said, "I know your deeds, your love and faith, your service and perseverance, and that you are now doing more than you did at first. Nevertheless I have this against you…" (Revelation 2:19). Now the tone changes. Outward conduct may be exemplary, but we can't fool Him. His burning eyes pierce the darkness and flash with the flame of moral anger.

Joseph Seiss wrote: "There is nothing more piercing than flaming fire. Everything yields and melts before it. It penetrates all things, consumes every opposition, sweeps down all obstructions, and presses its way with invincible power. And of this sort are the eyes of Jesus. They look through everything; they pierce through all masks and coverings; they search the remotest recesses; they behold the most hidden things of the soul; and there is no escape from them."[6]

In many ways, the service of Thyatira was better than that of the previous churches. Thyatira had the love that Ephesus had abandoned; the believers there preserved the faith that was in jeopardy in Pergamos and shared with Smyrna the patience needed to endure suffering. Instead of backsliding, the church was going forward. However, in the beautiful body of this church, a cancer was allowed to grow.

John Stott has reminded us of Satan's strategy: "If the devil cannot conquer the church by the application of political pressure or the propagation of intellectual heresy, he will try the insinuation of moral evil. This was the dragon's strategy in Thyatira."[7]

Lounging seductively behind the facade of piety was "that woman Jezebel." The real Jezebel had been dead for nearly a thousand years, but her prototype was a prophetess who had become prominent in Thyatira.

Historically, Jezebel was the wife of Ahab, one of Israel's most wicked kings. When she married Ahab, she brought her brand of religion with her and persuaded her husband to build a temple to Astarte, the goddess whose religion made sexual immorality a part of "worship."

Jezebel (and what little girl is ever given that infamous name today?) supported over 800 prophets of her immoral cult and killed all the prophets of Jehovah that she could find. Weak-kneed old Ahab didn't have the spiritual courage to stop his wicked wife. Jezebel's character was so evil that Elijah the prophet prophesied she would come to a sudden end and her body would be eaten by dogs. Jezebel was the epitome of immorality and idolatry.

Thyatira tolerated a satanic woman in its midst and refused to censor her. The Christians in Thyatira had either a poor conscience or very weak courage; their refusal to rebuke their Jezebel was like Ahab's refusal to deal with his.

Christ, always patient and desiring people to turn from their wicked ways, gave this adulterous woman time to repent, but she refused. He issued a dire warning; His message to the cult was severe. He said He would "cast her on a bed of suffering, and I will make those who commit adultery with her suffer intensly, unless they repent of her ways" (Revelation 2:22).

Literal punishments of sickness and death were to be inflicted upon the spiritual children of this cultic family. This truth about our Lord ought to be a sobering reminder that He looks past the facade and sees us for what we are.

Not everyone in the church of Thyatira had become a part of this evil cult; to this group of Christians, Christ gives some marvelous promises. He tells them to hold on to their faith until He returns.

It's encouraging to know that a remnant of this type of church will rule someday with Christ in His earthly kingdom. Hope is always present in the midst of the worst circumstances!

Sardis: The Liberal Church

A certain minister had a reputation for being eccentric. One Sunday morning, he told his congregation that he believed his church was dead. You can imagine the murmurings from the pews when he said, "Come back tonight, I'm going to preach the funeral service of the church." The members were shocked; the attendance for the evening service was larger than it had been in years.

In front of the pews was a casket and as the people sat in stunned silence, the pastor delivered the message. After the last "amen," the pastor said, "Some of you may not agree with me that this church is dead. So that you may be convinced, I am going to ask you to view the remains. I want you to file by the casket, one by one, and see who is dead."

In preparation for this unorthodox presentation, the minister had placed a mirror in the bottom of the casket. It is obvious who everyone saw when he came to view the deceased.

I would not recommend this technique, but the point is effective.

No Praise for Cold Sardians

This letter had a different tone from previous letters. For the poor, but rich, church in Smyrna, our Lord had nothing but words of praise. For the churches of Ephesus, Pergamos, and Thyatira, He had a mixture of praise and criticism. To the majority of the church as Sardis, He said nothing praiseworthy. Sardis may have been the first church in history to have been filled with what we call "nominal Christians." Sardis appeared to be alive, but was dead. The Lord is never impressed by the beauty of a well-kept mausoleum, knowing that inside are the bones of a dead man.

When John wrote this letter to Sardis, it was a wealthy city, but degenerate. Twice the city had been lost because the leadership and the citizenry were too lazy to defend themselves from their enemies. The attitude of the city was reflected in the demise of its church. Like the city that smugly dwelt upon its past glory, the church at Sardis had won a good reputation at one time and the members thought they had arrived; they were content in the beautiful building they had erected on the corner of Self-satisfaction and Complacency streets.

"I know your deeds; you have a reputation of being alive, but you are dead" (Revelation 3:1), Jesus wrote.

A spiritual autopsy of Sardis will show us the causes of death.

First, Sardis died because it relied on its past successes. The body which was once healthy had been neglected. Second, the church died because it allowed sin to creep into the membership. Herodotus, the historian, records that over the course of many years the church in Sardis had acquired a reputation for lax moral standards. Third, the church died because it was not sensitive to its own spiritual condition; it was confident that God was there because the building was magnificent and the parishioners were well-dressed. They were like the people Paul described in his letter of young Timothy: "...having a form of godliness but denying its power" (2 Timothy 3:5).

John Stott reminds us that hypocrisy like this can permeate the whole life of a church:

> "We can have a fine choir, an expensive organ, good music, great anthems, and fine congregational singing. We can mouth hymns and psalms with unimpeachable elegance, while our mind wanders and our heart is far from God. We can have pomp and ceremony, color and ritual, liturgical exactness and ecclesiastic splendor, and yet be offering a worship which is not perfect or 'fulfilled' in the sight of God."[8]

What Can We Do If Our Church Is Dead?

The letter to Sardis says, "Wake up!" Shake out of your smug, brick-walled, stained-glass complacency. Christ is not just saying to the church to wake from its death sleep, He is calling upon it to remain awake.

The first call toward renewal is the honest awareness that something is wrong. Churches die spiritually because Christians allow doctrinal error to slip into the membership. I've often had someone say, "Why do we have membership classes or examination of our beliefs before we're allowed to join a church? Anyone who wants to join should be allowed to do so." What if a teacher who believes in evolution becomes a member without any profession of faith? The Sunday school superintendent, eager to have a teacher for the fourth through six grades, asks the new member to take the classes. What are those children going to be taught?

Doctrine not important? It's vital.

Christ's warning to the church is sobering: "But if you do not wake up, I will come like a thief, and you will not know at what time I will come to you" (Revelation 3:3). I believe this is warning against the sudden judgment which God would bring upon this individual church if it did not watch and repent.

However, in the church at Sardis, and in our own Sardian-type churches today, there are a few who have remained true to Christ. There is never a day so dark that God does not have His stars—His men. In the days before the flood, God had righteous Enoch and Noah. In the time of universal idolatry, there was Abraham. Even in Sodom, there was Lot.

What should we do if we are members of a dead or dying church? Christ reminds the true believer of the importance of the Holy Spirit, to be submissive to His control. Some will be led out of that church, others will remain and hold fast.

Should I Stay or Should I Leave?

In the ancient city of Sardis there may not have been another Christian church, dead or alive. Today, believers have choices. For those within the church at Sardis who were true to Christ, a three-fold promise was given.

First, they would be dressed in white. In their Roman culture, this was significant, for they would have been reminded of the day of Roman triumph, when true Roman citizens donned the white toga and joined in a majestic triumphal procession. Christ reminded the believers in Sardis that they would walk one day in triumph with Christ. Next, He said that He would never blot out their names from the heavenly register and finally they would be acknowledged by Christ before the Father and His angels. Those are lofty promises, and I can imagine some of those faithful ones reading and re-reading that letter eagerly, being sustained during times when it looked the darkest.

Have you ever been in a dead church? It is like going to a funeral, only many sitting in the cold pews don't realize that rigor mortis has set in.

A news story quoted the Reverend Daniel Weis comparing "mainline Protestantism to the Prophet Ezekiel's vision of a 'valley of dead, dry bones.'" He added that "these bones can live... through our transformation as a people revitalized by the Spirit."[9]

Philadelphia: The Missionary Church

Of all the churches, this is the one you may remember because its name is familiar. If I had been a first-century man, the church at Philadelphia is where I would have liked to have my membership. I some ways, Philadelphia reminds me of where I live, in San Diego County, because it was frequently shaken by earthquakes. (However, that's not the reason I would have wanted to live there.)

Like Smyrna, Philadelphia had no word of condemnation. This church had right doctrine and right living going hand in hand. Where doctrine is present, without love, it is legalism; where love is present without doctrine, it is humanism.

God promised to open doors for this loving church, to give it an opportunity to reach out to a lost world. Christ was (and is) the great door-opener. This is an exciting and reassuring thing to know, because it is God, the Holy Spirit, who prepares the hearts of men to receive the Good News—not our plans, tracts, crusades, or feeble witnessing. Sometimes we defeat our personal witness by plunging in unceremoniously through a closed door. I know, because in my youthful zeal I have done just that. If the door is shut, don't put your shoulder to it and try to break it down!

The Philadelphian church was commended because it had "little strength." This is contrary to our human thinking, for we think we must be men and women of steel and iron to get God's work accomplished. We may be part of the 20 percent in the church who run the Sunday school, lead the choir, head the committees, and give the money. When we know that God has said, "My grace is sufficient for you, for power is perfected in weakness" (2 Corinthians 12:9), we can be sustained. When we are depending on buildings, budgets, staffs, organizational plans, and outreach, under our own power, we might as well be a business organization, rather than a church.

When a church is truly a church of the open door to the leading of His Holy Spirit, then watch out world! It is not enough to have the truth or right doctrine. These will die if we don't go through the open door. Churches that have vibrant missions and believe God for great things will reach out to the world.

In church history, the period of great missionary outreach, from 1750 until around 1925, was exemplified by the Church of Philadelphia. This was the era of Hudson Taylor, John Wesley, George Whitfield, Charles Haddon Spurgeon, D. L. Moody, and many more. The Salvation Army was founded; a whole galaxy of home missionary agencies sprung up. It was a time of great spiritual awakening.

Prophetic Promises to Philadelphia—And to Us

Wonderful promises are made to this church, promises that are key to understanding prophecy. First, He promises that there is an open door for believers to reach out to a lost world. We don't have to be eloquent or slick, we just need to be prayerfully available to His leading. What a comforting thought for timid souls who love the Lord, but have not had a course in "how to lead someone to Christ."

Listen to this! It stirs me to the core to have the Lord promise: "Since you have kept my command to endure patiently, I will also keep you from the hour of trial that is going to come upon the world" (Revelation 3:10). The Lord has a special plan that will keep the Philadelphia church (and all true believers) from the world-wide tribulation which is to come!

The "hour of trial" is the Great Tribulation. Notice He does not say, "I will keep you *through* the hour of trial," but *"from* the hour of trial." This refers to the Rapture, when Jesus will catch away God's people for Himself. We are pre-Tribulational in our beliefs, and we clearly see in this promise that the church will not go through the Tribulation. How can the clarity of this promise be explained any other way?

Notice that in chapters one through three of Revelation the church is mentioned nineteen times. After chapter four the Tribulation is described, but the church is not mentioned.

There are three positions on the Rapture, and we had better know what we believe or we will be shaken by every headline, every catastrophe, and every apostasy of our day. First there is the pre-Tribulational view which says all true believers will be raptured before the Tribulation begins. Second, there is the view that the church will be raptured in the middle of the Tribulation, or as the Great Tribulation begins. Third, some believe we will live through the Tribulation and be raptured and go up with the Lord at the end.

I know a man who was the pastor of a very large, evangelical church and on one occasion he said, "If I'm gone when the Tribulation begins, then I'm pre-Trib; if I stay around for three and a half years and then I'm raptured, I'm mid-Trib; if I live through the Tribulation, then I'm post-Trib. Whatever happens, I'm pan-Trib—everything will pan out all right."

While this may be humorous, unfortunately he is wrong, and he is denying his flock the assurance of the blessed hope.

An old Southern preacher said, "It's time for our church to wake up and sing up, preach up and pray up and never give up or let up or back up or shut up, until the church is filled up or we go up. Amen."

In every church today there are those who could have been members of the church of Ephesus, that had lost its first love or of Smyrna, the suffering ones. Modern members of Pergamum attend where Satan has his foothold. Thyatiran church-goers are weighted down with sexual sin while the Sardians are among the walking dead. The Philadelphians are filled with love. In fact, at different times we may posses the qualities of several of these churches.

As the historical time line of these churches approaches our era, there is a church which will be on earth when Christ returns. Is this the church of the latter part of the twentieth century? If so, it's later than we think.

THE LUKEWARM CHURCH IN THE LAST DAYS

What is the meaning of life? People with varied backgrounds were asked that question and one view was expressed by a taxi driver who said, "We're here to die, just live and die. Life is a big fake. Nobody gives a damn. You're rich or you're poor. You're here, you're gone. You're like the wind. After you're gone, other people will come. We're gonna destroy ourselves, nothing we can do about it. The only cure for the world's illness is nuclear war—wipe everything out and start over."[10]

Hopelessness is the saddest expression of man's feelings. Without hope we may exist, but we do not live.

The church should be the place where the present hope of Jesus Christ and the future hope of His return to establish His kingdom is proclaimed. Is this happening in every church today?

Within some churches who claim His name, are those who say that Christ's kingdom can be established here on earth during His absence. This movement takes various names: kingdom, dominion, reconstruction. The basic premise is that mortal man can accomplish what only the immortal Lord can perform. They believe that society must be reconstructed by Christians to establish the kingdom of God on earth before the personal return of Jesus Christ. Although this is a simplification of all the views espoused by the exponents of dominion theology, I believe they are removing the fire from evangelicalism and replacing it with dying embers. Their understanding of end-time prophecies is lacking.

A leading exponent of kingdom (or dominion) theology says, "...the kingdoms of this world must be steadily transformed into the kingdom of Christ...this historical transfer of kingdom ownership to Christ is to be made manifest in history."[11]

Today there are many Christians who are bent on changing society through government programs, lobbying activities, civil disobedience, and pressure groups. I do not find any place in the Bible that says this is the mission of the church of Jesus Christ. The mission of the church is witnessing to lost souls about the redemption provided by the Lord Jesus Christ. This mission is being replaced by those who believe the kingdom of God can be established here and now by our human activities.

Jesus warned that in the last days before His return there would be a church which would brag about its growing strength and self-importance. Today there are many undiscerning Christians who are looking for the kingdom of God on earth, a kingdom where justice will reign and nations will exist in peaceful coexistence. This arrogant church covets political power, not the power of God. The revival we have sought seems so slow in coming, that many believe Christians should take over the reins of government and legislate righteousness. Even the halls of Congress echo with a pharisaic piety, demanding outward vows of morality from its members.

I've asked myself these hard questions: "Would the history of nearly 2,000 years of the church of Jesus Christ have been changed if the martyrs during the era of the Roman caesars had overturned the despotic rulers? What would have happened in Babylon if Daniel had wrested the reins of government from Nebuchadnezzar? Would John have received and written the Revelation of Jesus Christ in a plush office in Laodicea, rather than the rocky desolation of Patmos? Are today's Christians convinced that placard-carrying, slogan-bearing demonstrators can replace soul-winners?

There *is* a better world coming, but not until those left on earth experience a time of evil fiercer than this planet has ever seen.

As an American who believes our country is the greatest, I want to do everything I can to fight injustice, and I support political candidates whose views are closest to biblical truths. However, I am dismayed to see what has happened in our generation to draw the church away from its central task.

Another direction is being taken by some Christian leaders to join with cultists to form a coalition for what they call "Christian causes." One group of American clergymen joined with Sun Myung Moon, the man who claims to be the second Messiah, to lobby for political candidates. How can the witness of the church be strengthened by these activities?

I believe we must be wary of the associations we form and the causes we champion.

Richard Halverson, past esteemed chaplain of the U.S. Senate, said, "The more I listen to evangelicals talk, the less I hear about the hope of Christ's coming again and the more I hear about making the USA a Christian nation, a prosperous nation...sometimes I think if Christ would come back, it would constitute a terrible interruption of their plans."[12]

A Look Inside the Last Church on Earth

The final church mentioned in Revelation is the lukewarm church of Laodicea, the church which will be in existence when Christ returns. I believe the majority of churches in these final days of the twentieth century are lukewarm. Let's look at the similarities between the organized Christian community today and the Laodicean church.

The church which received the last letter from the postman at

Patmos was outwardly impressive. It had all the trappings of wealth, but something was missing.

Under Roman rule, the city of Laodicea had become widely known for its banking establishments, medical school, and textile industry. However, with all this affluence, the church had been lulled to sleep. The members were rich in material goods, but spiritually poor. The Lord had nothing positive to say about this church; in fact, it made Him sick. It's interesting that God looks at apostasy and gets angry—but He looks at indifference and becomes ill.

The preaching in the church was compromising. The pastor probably didn't want to upset his congregation. Maybe he rattled their consciences a little—just enough to bring out the guilt and fill the collection plate, but what he wanted to hear after the service was, "That was a wonderful sermon, pastor. I enjoyed it very much."

The Lord says, "…because you are lukewarm—neither hot nor cold—I am about to spit you out of my mouth" (Revelation 3:16).

This is the only place in the New Testament where the word "lukewarm" is used. The expression is drawn from the geography of the area that surrounded the city. In the district of Hierapolis were hot mineral springs, whose water was transported to Laodicea in conduits. By the time it reached the city, it was no longer hot. Cold water was piped to Laodicea from Colossae, and it, too, would be lukewarm by the time it arrived. Lukewarm is the same as allowing coffee to cool and lemonade to warm.

In the Bible there are three possible heart temperatures: the *burning heart*: "…were not our hearts burning within us while he talked with us on the road and opened the Scriptures to us?"

(Luke 24:32); the *cold heart:* "Because of the increase of wicked-ness, the love of most will grow cold" (Matthew 24:12); and the *lukewarm heart* of the last church.

John Stott wrote: "The Laodicean church was a halfhearted church. Perhaps none of the seven letters is more appropriate to the twentieth-century church than this. It describes vividly the respectable, sentimental, nominal, skin-deep religiosity which is so widespread among us today. Our Christianity is flabby and anemic. We appear to have taken a lukewarm bath of religion."[13]

We are so afraid of being on fire for Christ; we don't want to be labeled as fanatics or extremists, yet in every other area of life we shed our proper manners and exude enthusiasm. I've shouted myself hoarse at a football or basketball game, and clapped until my hands were red for a talented singer or musician. Emerson said that nothing great was ever achieved without enthusiasm, but much of our Christian experience is as limp as an overcooked noodle.

I remember hearing of an eccentric man who walked around town with a sandwich sign slung over his shoulders. The front of the sign said: "I am a fool for Christ's sake." As he strolled the streets, he was ridiculed by those who saw the front of his plac-ard, until he walked by and they read what was written on the back: "Whose fool are you?"

The lukewarm Laodicean church was conceited: "You say, 'I am rich; I have acquired wealth and do not need a thing.' But you do not realize that you are wretched, pitiful, poor, blind, and naked" (Revelation 3:17).

The wealthy banking city had squeezed the church into its mold; the spirit of the marketplace had crept in and values became twisted. The church was proud of its ministry because it used the human measuring standard, instead of the divine.

David Wilkerson, author of *The Cross and the Switchblade*, commented: "Jesus clearly warned that a church would evolve in the last days of civilization which would boast that it was rich, growing, increasing in numbers, and self-sufficient… For nearly two thousand years the church of Jesus Christ has been rejected and persecuted by the world. The blood of millions of rejected martyrs cries out from the ground. The Bible says they all died in faith and the world was not worthy of them. Am I now to believe that Jesus has changed his mind and has decided to close out the ages with a lukewarm, rich, pampered, boastful, self-centered church? Will the last army of God consist of precinct workers getting out the vote? Will the soul-winners be replaced with petitioners going into the highways and hedges seeking signatures for some social cause?"[14]

The Great Physician's Prescription for a Sick Body

Some people think they don't need a doctor. "I can take care of myself, nobody needs to tell me what to do," boasts the self-sufficient man. Then comes the gripping pain in the chest, a shortness of breath, and the gasping plea, "Call a doctor!" The fellow recovers, but not until a physician gives him some strong admonitions about a change in lifestyle.

Christ gave us specific prescriptions for the sick church of the end times. He wrote them out clearly, so that anyone could read the directions. First He said, "Those whom I love I rebuke and discipline. So be earnest, and repent" (Revelation 3:19).

Notice that He didn't say, "Think about it," or "When you get around to it," but do it now! The weakness of compromise must be replaced by the humility of repentance.

Another prescription was given for the church's spiritual poverty. He told the people they must no longer trust in their banks, but come to Christ for His riches. The Laodiceans were well endowed with the riches of this earth, but what they really needed they could not buy with their gold.

If a person walked down the street stark naked, he would be arrested and carted off to jail or a mental institution. The Laodiceans were like the emperor in Hans Christian Andersen's story; they thought they were clothed in splendor, when they were really naked! Christ wanted to clothe them in "white clothes to wear, so you can cover your shameful nakedness" (Revelation 3:18).

The idea of spiritual nakedness in the Bible refers to being spiritually defeated and humiliated. White clothes (or fine linen, clean and white) symbolize the righteous acts of believers. The lukewarm lifestyle of the Laodicean church needed to be transformed into a lifestyle of red hot zeal for God.

The next prescription was for the cure of spiritual blindness. Revelation 3:18 refers to "salve to put on your eyes, so you can see."

In the city of Laodicea there was a medical school. One of the medicinal products manufactured and exported from that medical center was a tablet that was sold all over the Roman Empire. This tablet was used to heal a wide range of eye ailments: the instructions said to crush the tablet, mix it with a small amount of water, rub it on the eyes, and wait for the healing. Jesus reminded the blind Laodiceans that they needed more than their precious eye salve to see; they needed the truth of God which only Christ could bring them.

It makes me think of the spiritual blindness of New Agers and

Reconstructionists, whose vision is so sadly blinded, or the church-goers who "enjoy" the sermon and the music, and leave without any change of heart.

The final prescription is a positive cure for compromise, poverty, nakedness, and blindness. The greatest invitation in the Bible is contained in Revelation 3:20: "Here I am! I stand at the door and knock. If anyone hears my voice and opens the door, I will come in and eat with him, and he with me."

When Jesus came the first time He was not received by His own people (John 1:11). During His first visit to this planet, Christ predicted that His second coming would also be met with unbelief (Luke 18:8).

The condition of the church at the time of Christ's return is Christless. Notice He says, "if *anyone* hears my voice…I will come in." While the hierarchy in many end-time churches has denied Christ entrance to their organizations, He still knocks at the door of each person's heart.

God does not force Himself upon anyone. No one is saved against his will; no one is compelled to obedience who wants to be rebellious. Notice that this invitation is extended to the last church ever mentioned in the Bible. That fact grips me with urgency for our day.

Campbell Morgan said:

"The only cure for lukewarmness is the readmission of the excluded Christ. Apostasy must be confronted with His fidelity, looseness with conviction born of His authority, poverty with the fact of His wealth, frost with the mighty fire of His enthusiasm, and death with the life divine that is in His gift. There is no other cure for the malady of the world, for the lukewarmness of the Church than the readmitted Christ."[15]

The Church at the Crossroads

Seven churches have been described in this last book of the Bible. In our present age we may have difficulty seeing ourselves as belonging to any of these churches; however, some of their characteristics are found in each one of us.

The church at Ephesus was once strong, but it had lost its first love. It had become lifeless, forgetting the passion and excitement of its original love for Jesus.

The church at Smyrna was a suffering church, enduring hardship for its faith.

The church at Pergamum had fallen under the influence of the pagan culture in which it lived.

The church at Thyatira had become part of an evil cult.

The Sardian church was so cold and dead that only the names in the church directory could have indicated any living members.

The church in Philadelphia was a loving church, the one for which the Lord had no negative words.

Finally, we have visited the weak, lukewarm church of Laodicea.

Why are there no more letters to other churches? What happened to the church of Jesus Christ after the Laodicean era? Did it disappear?

If we are living in that time of the last church on earth before Christ's return, what other signs are pointing toward that cataclysmic event?

The hour hand on God's time clock is wound up and spinning. We are being swept along the path of history by a swift wind at our backs. Our individual ability to weather the storm will come from our understanding of the Word of God. We need only heed what has echoed through the centuries: "He who has an ear, let him hear what the Spirit says to the churches" (Revelation 3:22).

1. Charles Haddon Spurgeon. Sermon Notes.

2. Marcus L. Loane, *They Overcame* (Grand Rapids: Eerdmans, 1937), 41.

3. Corrie ten Boom, *Marching Orders for the End Times,* (London: Christian Literature Crusade, 1969), 83, 86.

4. Sergui Grossu, *The Church in Today's Catacombs* (New Rochelle, NY: Arlington House Publishers, 1975), 57.

5. Accounts taken from *Eerdmans Handbook to the History of Christianity* (Berkhamsted, Herts, England: Leon Publishing, 1977), 81.

6. J. A. Seiss, *The Apocalypse, Lectures on the Book of Revelation* (Grand Rapids: Zondervan, 1964).

7. John R. W. Stott, *What Christ Thinks of the Church* (Grand Rapids: Eerdmans, 1958), 72.

8. Ibid., 88.

9. *Los Angeles Times,* Part II, 4 March 1989, 7.

10. Brian Lanker, "The Meaning of Life," *Life,* December 1988.

11. Gary North, *Liberating Planet Earth* (Fort Worth, TX: Dominion Press, 1987), 9.

12. Richard Halverson, quoted in *The Omega Letter* (North Bay, Ontario, Canada, February 1989), 4.

13. John Stott, *What Christ Thinks of the Church,* 116.

14. David Wilkerson, "The Laodicean Lies!" *Evangelist* magazine, December 1986, 15–17.

15. G. Campbell Morgan, *The Letters of Our Lord* (Old Tappan, NJ: Fleming H. Revell), 108.

THE APOSTLE PAUL ANNOUNCED HIS COMING IN THE AIR

CHARLES C. RYRIE

Charles C. Ryrie, Th.D., Ph.D., General Editor, Ryrie Study Bible
Professor of systematic theology emeritus
Dallas Theological Seminary
Author of more than thirty books

The last words of a dying friend are always full of meaning, and the last words of the Lord Jesus are no exception. The scene in the Upper Room on the night of His betrayal, just before the Crucifixion, was packed with emotion. The Lord had just announced His betrayal by Judas, and His impending death (John 13:21, 31). This would involve, He said, His leaving the disciples (v. 33). As usual, Peter reacted first—in this case with a question. "Where will you go?" he asked. "And why can I not follow You, wherever it be?"

Against this background, the Bible gives us God's first revelation bearing on the tremendous event which we call the Lord's return.

There are many Christians who believe that Christ's return is one single event—that the Lord will return bodily to this earth and establish His kingdom. Many evangelical believers, however, are convinced that the Lord will return in two "stages"—that first He will return "in the air" and take His people out of the world, and that later He will return "with His saints" to set up His thousand-year kingdom. These believers refer to the first state of Christ's coming as the "Rapture [taking away] of the church."

His Parting Promise

It is not hard to imagine the feeling that the disciples must have had when they heard that their Lord was going to leave them, and when, as far as they knew, there would never be any prospect of their seeing Him again. To comfort them, the Lord said, "In My Father's house are many mansions: if it were not so, I would have told you. I go to prepare a place for you. And if I go and prepare a place for you, I will come again, and receive you unto Myself; that where I am, there ye may be also" (John 14:2–3).

As a good bridegroom, the Lord announced His intention to prepare a dwelling place for His bride (the word *mansion* is better translated "dwelling place," like a single apartment in a large apartment complex). And, as a good bridegroom, He wants His bride with Him, so He assured the disciples that He would return to take them to be with Himself.

It is important to notice that all the Lord promised on this occasion was the simple fact that He would return for His followers—that they would see Him again. There is no elaboration of this promise. Christ did not say anything about *when* or *how* His coming would occur, but you can easily imagine what comfort He brought to the disciples, even though they could not know, at that time, all that was included in this parting promise.

A Mystery Solved

To most people, a mystery is something unintelligible—unless you know the secret of it! In Greek, the word "mystery" was used of the sacred rites of the Greek mystery religions—secrets shared only by those who had been initiated into the religion. Equivalent words in other languages sometimes indicate that a mystery is some kind of deep or high wisdom, far above finite understanding. Therefore, the word "mystery" includes the idea of something secret and of something containing deep truth.

In the New Testament, a "mystery" is a secret which has always been in the plan or purpose of God but which He has not revealed until a certain point in time.

What does this concept of a mystery have to do with the Rapture of the church? Though the Greeks believed in the immortality of the soul, they did not accept the resurrection of the body. Their thinking had affected some Christians at Corinth, so Paul wrote to them to correct their view (1 Corinthians 15). He declared not only that Christ had been raised from the dead, but that all men will also someday be raised. This was not new teaching, for Christ Himself had taught the same thing. He had said that all who are in the grave will someday hear His voice and be raised, some to life and some to condemnation (John 5:26–29).

In writing to the Corinthians, Paul used the word "mystery" (1 Corinthians 15:51). The work is like a red flag signaling that something hitherto unknown is about to be revealed. And the secret that is here made known is the fact that not everyone will die. The Old Testament had revealed that men would be raised from the dead (Job 19:25; Isaiah 26:19; Daniel 12:2), but it had given no hint that anybody could come into God's presence without going through death and resurrection. To be sure, Enoch and Elijah had both experienced translation. That is, they had been given glorified bodies without their dying. But there was no promise that this means would be used for anyone else. That is why this newly revealed promise, "We shall not all sleep," is called a *mystery*.

A popular radio commentator, when reporting someone's death always said, "As it must to all men, death came today to…" His theology was poor, for all men will not die. There is another route into God's presence, the way of translation.

Both routes, death and translation, involve a change. Paul goes on to explain the two changes. The one will be experienced by those who have died in the Lord. Since their bodies will have seen corruption, they must put on incorruption at the resurrection of the body. But those who are living at the Lord's coming will not have died; their bodies will not have seen corruption. Therefore they will experience a different means of change. Since they will be mortal, they need only to put on immortality. This new route into God's presence is the truth that is revealed in this mystery. The dead will need resurrection, but the living will only need change (1 Corinthians 15:52). God will effect this change for all living believers when the Lord comes. The last generation of Christians will not experience death.

How quickly will these two changes occur—the resurrection of dead saints and the translation of living believers? Paul says it will all happen "in a moment, in the twinkling of an eye." The whole procedure will be instantaneous, not gradual! The Greek word translated "moment" is the term from which our word *atom* comes. Because when the atom was discovered it was thought to be indivisible, it was named "atom." Even though it has been split, the term *atom* still means "indivisible." Here it indicates that the Rapture (including both dead and living saints) will take place in an indivisible instant of time.

The words "moment" and "twinkling" refer to the instantaneous nature of this event, and the phrase "at the last trump" reminds us of its finality. After the trumpet sounds, there will be no time to prepare, for the changes will occur instantly. There will be no second chance for those who, up till then, have refused the grace of God.

Paul says we shall *all* be changed in that instant. This would seem to disprove the teaching that only certain believers will be raptured, while others will be left to go through a partial rapture.

To sum up: expanding on the Lord's promise to come again, Paul revealed (1 Corinthians 15:51–57) four features of this event: (1) It will include not only the bodily resurrection of those believers who have died, but also the changing of the bodies of those who are alive at the time it happens. (2) It will be instantaneous. (3) It will be final. (4) It will include *all* believers, not simply *some* of them.

None Left Out

As in the church at Corinth, there was a problem in the church at Thessalonica, too. Early Christians in Thessalonica, like those elsewhere, expected the Lord to return within their lifetime, but He did not. In time some of them died. Those who remained thought that those who died had been robbed of sharing in the glorious reign of Christ. Paul's answer to the problem is a reassuring affirmation that the dead will certainly be raised and will therefore share in the kingdom. The apostle gives a detailed picture of this resurrection of believers, including the change that will at the same time take place in living believers.

Our assurance that all this will happen is based on our hope of sharing in the resurrection of Christ (vv. 13–14) and on the direct promise of the Word of the Lord (v. 15).

The certainty of a Christian's resurrection is based on the fact of Christ's rising. When the word "sleep," in the New Testament, is used of death, it is used only in relation to the death of believers—never of unbelievers. The object of this metaphor is to suggest that as a sleeper does not cease to exist while his body sleeps, so a dead believer continues to exist even if those who remain alive cannot communicate with him. Moreover, sleep is temporary, and so is the death of the body. Sleep ends in waking, death in resurrection.

Any sorrow which a Christian may have over the loss of a loved one (and it is comforting to remember that our Lord wept when His friend Lazarus died, John 11:33–35) is unlike the hopeless despair which unbelievers have.

Actually, Paul did *not* really say that Christians may sorrow, only not to the same degree as the heathen, for such an interpretation would strain the words, "even as." He said that Christians are *not* like the heathen because Christians *do not* sorrow. He did not deny that we grieve over loss (Philippians 2:27), but that is not the point here.

Our assured hope is based on our preview of resurrection, as seen in the resurrection of Christ. The "if" (1 Thessalonians 4:14) does not express doubt, and it may be translated "since." The resurrection of Christ *guarantees* the resurrection of Christians.

By contrast, here is an example of the hopelessness of the heathen in the face of death, from a letter written in the second century: "Eirene to Taonnophris and Pilon, good cheer! I was as much grieved and shed as many tears over Eumoiros as I shed for Didymas, and I did everything that was fitting, and so did my whole family...but still there is nothing one can do in the face of such trouble. So I leave you to comfort yourselves. Good-bye."

After the preview comes a promise (v. 15), and the statement is made as authoritative as possible by the declaration that it is the Word of the Lord. Another detail is added: the dead will have first place. At the Lord's coming, those who are living will not precede those who have died. Paul included himself ("we") among the living group. Evidently he expected to live until the return of Christ. This is one of the wonderful things about the hope of Christ's coming—it is equally bright for each generation, regardless of how long it seems to be delayed.

What will happen when the Lord returns? Five features are spotlighted:

1. *Christ will return* (v. 16). He Himself, not an emissary or agent whom He might send in His place, will come for His people. Because He Himself will come, the attendant circumstances will include all the grandeur His personal presence deserves.

There will be a shout. This word of command is used in classical Greek for the shout with which an officer gave the order to his troops or his crew. There is in the term a ring of authority and a note of urgency. It is not said who utters the shout—whether it is the Lord or an archangel—but the voice of an archangel will be heard. Michael is the only archangel mentioned in the Bible by name (Jude 9), but it is not impossible that there are other archangels (see Daniel 10:13). The trumpet of God will also sound when Christ comes—a detail already noticed (1 Corinthians 15:52).

2. *There will be a resurrection* (v. 16). Again the priority of the dead is mentioned. They will be raised before those who are alive are changed. All will happen, however, in the twinkling of an eye. The group raised at this time is limited to those who are "in Christ." This indicated that not all the dead will be raised at the same time. The passage does not support the idea, so often heard,

of a "general resurrection." At this point, only dead *believers* will be made alive.

3. *The Rapture will occur* (v. 17). Living believers will be changed and "caught up to be with the Lord." The word "caught up" means to "seize" or to "snatch," and this verb, in Latin, is the term from which we get the English word "rapture." Strictly speaking, the word *rapture* means the act of conveying a person from one place to another, and is properly used of the taking of living persons to heaven. Paul used it of his own experience of being caught up into the third heaven (2 Corinthians 12:4). However, we use the term, "rapture of the church" loosely to include all that happens at Christ's coming, including not only the change in living Christians but also the resurrection of dead believers. The term "rapture" implies whatever change is necessary to fit mortal bodies for immortal existence in heaven. Though the method of this change is nowhere explained, Paul clearly believed that it is possible to have such a metamorphosis without Christians experiencing the dissolution caused by death and the grave.

4. *There will be a reunion* (v. 17), and it will be twofold. Living Christians will be reunited with loved ones who have died, for they shall be caught up together with them. But even more wonderful will be the reunion of the church with the Lord. Both these reunions will be forever!

5. *This truth is a constant reassurance to all believers* (v. 18). They need not sorrow over those who have died. Comfort and hope are the logical consequences of this glorious truth.

We often hear of the "secret rapture." This term is misleading, for though the time of the event is unknown, the effect will be openly observed anywhere there were Christians before its occurrence. Newspaper headlines and radio and TV reports on the news will "cover" this event, or at least the results of it. Some places will be almost or entirely unaffected by the removal of living Christians because there will be few or no believers there.

It is rather intriguing to speculate on what explanation TV commentators will give on the day the Rapture takes place. Undoubtedly they will try to give "rational" and "reasonable" appraisals that leave the Bible out. However, some people will remember hearing the Rapture preached on, or will turn to their Bibles and read God's explanation. But no matter how people will try to explain it, the event will happen just as God, in His prophetic Word, has said it will.

They Don't Agree on the "When"

We have seen that there are several views concerning the time of the Lord's coming in relation to the Millennium. There are also differing viewpoints about the relation between His coming for the church and the time of the Tribulation, though this question is generally discussed only among premillenarians. Amillenarians believe there is only one future and final coming of Christ, followed immediately by the ushering in of eternity. Posmillennialists do not believe in a tribulation period at all, and in their view, Christ comes after the Millenium is over.

Premillennialists agree that at the conclusion of a time of tribulation on this earth (most concur that this period will be seven years long) the Lord will return and establish His millennial kingdom. They also agree that His coming for His own people is described as distinct and separate from His Second Coming. They disagree on *when* His coming for His own people will occur in relation to His second return to earth to set up His kingdom.

Posttribulationalists say that Christ's coming *for* His saints and

His coming *with* His saints will both occur in quick succession after the Tribulation.

Midtribulationists believe that Christ's coming for His people will happen at the middle point of the Tribulation period—that is, three and a half years before the time when the Lord returns with His people to set up His kingdom.

Pretribulationalists hold that the coming of Christ for His people will take place before the Tribulation begins at all, and that the church will escape the entire period of trouble here on the earth. Then, seven years later, after the Tribulation concludes, the Lord will return to earth with His redeemed people to set up His kingdom.

Those who believe in the pretribulation view of the Rapture support their position with two principal reasons:

1. The risen Lord promised the church at Philadelphia to "keep thee from the hour of temptation, which shall come upon all the world, to try them that dwell upon the earth" (Revelation 3:10). They apply this promise, like promises made in other letters to local churches, to the whole church (though obviously it will be experienced only by believers living when Christ comes), and they assume that the "hour of temptation" refers to the Tribulation.

Some people say this promise merely means that Christians will be protected from the plagues and persecutions of the Tribulation, though they will live *through* it—much as the Children of Israel were kept from the effects of some of the plagues in Egypt though they lived through them. But, of course, the promise is not only to keep *from* (and the preposition means *from*, not *in*) the trouble, but to keep from the *hour* (or time) of trouble. The promise to be kept from the hour of trouble would seem to imply

THE APOSTLE PAUL ANNOUNCED ...   189

exemption from being anywhere around when it took place. Since the Tribulation will be worldwide, such exemption could be given to living believers only by removing all of them from the earth before the trouble begins.

2. The Tribulation is called "the great day of His wrath" (Revelation 6:17). Believers, who know the Deliverer from the wrath to come (1 Thessalonians 1:10), are assured that God has not appointed them to wrath (5:9). Since in the context of this latter verse Paul is speaking about the *beginning* of the Tribulation period (5:2), it seems clear that he is saying that Christians will not be present during any part of the time of wrath, but will be removed before it begins. The pretribulation view seems to be more compatible with the concept of the Rapture as a comforting and blessed hope.

It Could Be Today

I believe that the Rapture of believers can occur at any time. Nothing is yet unfulfilled which must take place before believers are caught up to meet the Lord in the air.

There are two indications that the Rapture may be very close. One is the increase of apostasy in the organized church in the world today. Since these evidences seem to be increasing, we may say that the Rapture is nearer. They are in fact sufficiently present in the church today that one wonders how they could increase much before the Lord comes.

Apostasy is characteristic of the church throughout all of its history; increasing apostasy is a significant sign of the rapidly approaching end of human history as we know it.

We may also realize the nearness of His coming by comparing the Bible picture of times during the pretribulation days with conditions as they are today. If the trends, apostasy, alliances, and other characteristics of the Tribulation seem to be similar to those which exist today, we may safely conclude that the Tribulation is probably not far off. And if it is near, then so is the coming of the Lord.

By every indication which we can gauge, the Rapture seems near. Certainly each day that passes brings it 24 hours nearer, and each trend that develops points to its coming. God says that this is a blessed hope—at least it *will* be if we are ready to meet the Lord. If not, we should *get* ready and then know the joy of eagerly anticipating seeing Him whose coming will be "in the twinkling of an eye."

THE SIGNS
OF THE TIMES IMPLY
HIS COMING

TIM LAHAYE

Tim LaHaye, D.Min.
Director of Family Life Seminars
Author of numerous books

For 2000 years, Christians have believed Jesus Christ would return to this earth, physically, in his "second coming," in their generation. Even though Our Lord knew the church would not see that return for two millennia, He wanted each generation to live as though He could come at any time for motivational purposes. Our Lord knew He would "go into a far country. And after a great while…return and demand an accounting," as He taught in His parables. He knew that routine living was an enemy to spiritual motivation in a physical universe. So He presented His second coming in such a way that Christians would be motivated to so live as though He would interrupt their lives and return before their natural life span had ended.

The apostles and first century church universally expected His return in their lifetime, which is why they were so motivated to live holy lives and so dedicated to evangelism and reaching the world for Christ. The second and third century churches similarly expected His return, even in the face of unbelievable persecution. They were so evangelistic they literally turned the world upside down, and by the fourth century they saw the Roman empire embrace Christianity as the dominant faith. In later centuries, as the Bible was withdrawn from the people, the truth about the second coming waned, as did the fires of evangelism. After the Protestant Reformation, the translating of the Bible into the mother tongue of the people, and the printing press, which made the Bible available to the common people, the study of prophecy and the second coming resumed. After all, one third of the Bible is prophecy, so if you study the whole Bible you study prophecy. Since the second coming is mentioned more than any other subject in Scripture, except for the doctrine of salvation, it is understandable that prophetic teaching, followed by evangelism, missions, and holy living would return. Historically, that is exactly what happened during the last three centuries—as the Bible had its greatest distribution.

It is only natural that Bible-taught Christians, excited about Christ's return, would be interested in "signs" of His coming. Even the disciples, once they realized Jesus would soon leave, asked, "What shall be the Sign of your coming?" which they obviously equated with "the end of the age" (Matthew 24:3). The fact that the Lord did not rebuke the disciples for their question tells us that it was a legitimate one. It is equally legitimate today. That many wild speculators have sensationalized signs, and so brought confusion to the church, should not prohibit us from using them at all. It should make us more careful in "rightly dividing the Word of Truth," so we do not add to the confusion. Neither should we rob the church of legitimate motivation for holy living, evangelism, and missionary vision, by refusing to face the fact that there are many events today that constitute seeming fulfillment of certain prophecies.

We should, however, avoid speculations that go beyond the intent of Scripture, and not make them mean more than is indicated. Certainly we should avoid date-setting. The 1988 experience of the now discredited Edgar Whisenant, and the 1994 date setting of Harold Camping, do nothing to build confidence in the soon coming of Christ. Instead, they disillusion many. Any time a person sets a specific date we know he is wrong. According to our Lord's statement in Matthew 24:36, we cannot know "the day or the hour." However, in the same passage, He allows us to see indications that would lead us to believe "it is near, even at the doors."

It is my contention that, while we cannot say dogmatically that Jesus will return in our generation, we can say that our generation has more legitimate reasons for believing it than any previous generation. Consider the following 12 reasons carefully. No one of them is conclusive in itself, though number two comes close. But considered together, these 12 reasons for expecting the Savior to "shout from heaven" and rapture his church in our generation, should affect the way we live.

There Are More Fulfilled Signs Today Than in Any Previous Age

A whole book could be written on the signs of our Lord's return that have already been fulfilled. In fact, I have written such a book, *The Beginning of the End,* where I list 12 signs. Other students of prophecy have found more. The 12 I see as most specific are listed below with their Scripture text.

1) *World War I:* Matthew 24:1–8. Actually, there are 4 parts to this one sign: a world war started by one nation, joined by the

kingdoms of the world, followed by famines, pestilences, and earth-quakes in several places at the same time. This century has already been the most barbaric century in history, killing a record number of souls in two world wars and with the spread of communism. In excess of 180 million lives, more than all the wars of history put together, have been lost. In addition, over 5000 lives have been lost in earthquakes, famines, and pestilence in this generation.

2) *The Regathering of Israel:* Ezekiel 36–37. This is such a significant sign as you will see later.

3) *The Rise of Russia and Her Allies in Preparation of Fulfilling:* Ezekiel 38–39. Only in this century (since 1917) has Russia been anything like a dominant player on the world scene. This is a compelling sign worthy of individual study. Not only is Russia depicted clearly by Ezekiel to rise as a political threat in the last days, but her allies—the Arab nations—and her enemy—Israel—are named.

4) *The Increase in Travel and Knowledge:* Daniel 12:4. This is the "information age." Who can doubt the prophet's prediction of "running to and fro on the earth"?

5) *The Capital and Labor Conflicts:* James 5:1–6. These have produced revolutionary changes in labor and management during this century.

6) *Scoffers Have Come:* 2 Peter 3:1–2. This is a sign of the "last days." Scoffers dominate the most influential agencies of all countries today, even our own. They control media, entertainment, education, and, for the most part, government. They are "willfully ignorant" and "walk after their own lusts," as predicted.

7) *The Current Moral Breakdown in Society:* 2 Timothy 3:1–5. The 18 trends of moral breakdown during the last days are read almost every day in the newspapers.

8) *A Rise in Lawlessness:* 2 Thessalonians 2:7–10.

9) *A Rise in Occultism and Cults:* 1 Timothy 4:1–5. There have always been cults and demon activity, but nothing in modern history is like today, and it is increasing.

10) *Apostasy:* 1 Timothy 4:1. The liberalism and rejection of the faith that has shipwrecked so many souls in this century had its roots in the last century, as whole denominations departed from their original beliefs in the deity of Jesus Christ and other doctrines.

11) *The Rise of Mystery Babylon, the Ecumenical Church:* Revelation 17. Ever since the pagan practices of Babylon and other heathen religions began creeping into the church of Rome (mid fourth and fifth century), faithful Bible teachers have identified the church of Rome as the harlot riding the "beast" of government in Revelation 17. Today we even have evangelical leaders making attempts to reconcile with Rome, Babylon, a most dangerous trend, but to be expected in the light of the prophecy of Revelation.

12) *The One World Government:* Daniel 2. Many saw the establishment of the United Nations, in 1945, as a giant step in fulfilling the long-recognized prophecy of a one world government in the end times. The World Trade Organization (NAFTA) recently passed into law, the federating of the countries of Europe into the "United States of Europe." The World Trade Organization could well be fulfillment of the move toward a one-world government, just as Daniel prophesied.

A case can be made that each of the above events, or common trends of our day, are signs of our Lord's return, but as stated earlier, that in itself is a subject worthy of a book. It is significant to point out, here, that they all occurred in this century, and that they are working inexorably toward a climax that could well culminate in our generation. Together, they give us a basis for concluding that this generation has more reason to believe that Christ could come in our lifetime than at any time before it. Below we will expand on these ideas and look at others as well.

Israel's Regathering: The "Super Sign" of Christ's Return

Israel is a miracle nation. It was born by a miracle, it lived by a miracle, and it has been preserved by the miraculous hand of God all through history. That after 1500 years without a homeland this dispersed people could be gathered back into the holy land in this century, and recognized as an official nation in 1948, is itself a miracle. Historians tell us that no other nationality has been able to survive extinction after 500 years of being removed from its homeland. Yet, scattered as they were to all the world, with the signing of the Balfore Treaty in 1917, the miracle nation that we today call Israel began. They came from all over the world, until the handful of Jews in the holy land at the time of World War I, had grown until, today, there are almost five million Jews in that land, testifying that God keeps His Word.

A careful reading of Ezekiel 37 shows that God predicted a very gradual regathering of this seemingly dead nation. The prophet pictured the nation as in the "valley of dry bones," which, after the signal of the Lord, began coming together, "bone to its bone"…then the "sinews, flesh,"…then the…"skin," and finally the "breath" (world recognition in 1948). There is no doubt that the dry bones were the nation of Israel, for verse 11 says, "Son of Man, these bones are the whole house of Israel." Even though they thought, "Our bones are dry, our hope is lost and we ourselves are cut off!" God has brought them back into their land. It is a miracle!

Now all that is needed is for God to pour out His Spirit, so the nation can experience the spiritual revival that is predicted for her in verses 12–15 and other passages. But that is yet future. It is expected to occur during the Tribulation period, under the preaching of the 144,000 Jewish witnesses described in Revelation 7.

What is significant, here, is this "super sign." It all started in 1917, with the fulfillment of the sign our Lord gave His disciples in Matthew 24:6–7: World War I followed by unprecedented "famines, pestilences, and earthquakes in various places." Notice, "wars and rumors of wars" were not the sign. Man's history is filled with war after war, but Jesus said, "See that you are not troubled; for all these things must come to pass, but the end is not yet." The sign was not wars, but a most significant war, which was World War I, with its accompanying phenomena of famines, pestilences, and earthquakes. Out of the fulfillment of this sign, Israel started going back into the land, leading many prophecy scholars to conclude that God's prophetic clock began ticking again. Personally, I look on that period, 1917–1948, as God winding His clock. It was set in motion when President Harry Truman pushed through the United Nations the vote to recognize Israel as a nation and she rose up from the valley of dry bones and began to "live."

When you add to that fulfilled prophecy the next two chapters of Ezekiel, 38–39, which foretell the amazing story of how Russia and its Arab allies will (as Gog and Magog, Rosh and the prince of Rosh) go down against the mountains of Israel and be destroyed supernaturally by God, you are faced with the remarkable fact that it too began in 1917. That is when Russia became a mainstream player in the world of nations. Just 100 years ago, Russia was such a backward nation that it couldn't even best the newly emerging nation of Japan in 1905. Yet for decades Russia has been a dominant force on the world scene. And it is today a mortal enemy of Israel, just as the Bible predicted!

The Middle East: Focus of the World Attention

Has it ever seemed unusual to you that the focus of world attention is continually on the little nation of Israel? Even today they only have five million people in the land, plus Arabs, Palestinians, Syrians, and Jordanians. At one place the country is only eight miles wide, and it has all kinds of survival problems. Yet almost every night on the evening news, billions of people focus their attention on that tiny spot of land that God gave Abraham for a homeland, for the nation He would raise up through Abraham and his wife Sarah.

To put this in perspective, think of the country of Singapore. When I visited missionaries there some years back, one of them told me that Singapore was the center of world population. He said, "If you draw a two thousand mile wide circle around Singapore, you will encompass fifty percent of the world's population!" But how often do the happenings in that area of 50 percent of the world's population ever hit our evening news? Yet Israel is on the evening news regularly.

Why? Because God predicted, in those most important prophecies in Ezekiel 37–39, that Israel, Russia, and the Arab hordes would be the principle focus of world attention in the last days. It is significant that that was not the case in the last century or in the 19 centuries before it.

The Potential of Nuclear or Other Holocausts

For the first time in human history man has the potential of destroying himself from the face of the earth. Most scientists' greatest fear is that a nuclear device could be set off and cause a chain reaction that could obliterate the planet. *Psychology Today* magazine featured a cover design showing the typical mushroom like cloud of a nuclear explosion, titled "Children Growing Up with the Fear of Never Growing Up." Disarmament agents in education and media use this threat to advance their cause of universal disarmament, which only intensifies the fear, particularly among young school children, causing many in their youth to adopt the hedonistic lifestyle.

Christians do not share that concern. The Bible forecasts that Christ will come back and rapture His church at a time of enormous population. He will not only take many to be with Him to His Father's house, but He will leave behind multitudes more to go through the Tribulation. This world will one day be destroyed, but it will be destroyed by God, not man, after the return of Christ for His church.

Former president Ronald Reagan is quoted as saying, "We see around us today the marks of a terrible dilemma, predictions of doomsday. Those predictions carry weight because of the existence of nuclear weapons, and the constant threat of global war…so much so that no president, no congress, no parliament can spend a day entirely free of this threat." Not only do they fear rogue nations, which would threaten other more civilized nations to surrender to them to avoid nuclear holocaust, making world domination by another Joe Stalin-type possible, there is always the threat of nuclear proliferation by some terrorist group which, if they could develop a delivery system, would blackmail cities or countries with annihilation.

That possibility is not as farfetched as some people think. Recently, a news report indicated that a nuclear device had been developed that could fit into a briefcase. It is just a matter of time before this frightening scenario from science fiction becomes reality.

Nuclear weapons or explosives are not the only technological threat to mankind today. Dr. George Wald, Nobel prize-winning scientist, and biology department head at Harvard University, is quoted a saying, " I think human life is threatened as never before in the history of this planet. Not by one peril, but by many. They are all working together coming to a head about the same time. And the time lies very close to the year 2000. I am one of those scientists who find it hard to see how the human race is to bring itself much past the year 2000." French biologist, Dr. Jacques Monod, is only slightly more optimistic, "I don't see how we can survive much later than 2050.

My point is not to suggest that these doomsday prophecies will come to fulfillment in our lifetime, or before Christ returns. As we have seen, they most assuredly will not. My point is, since Christ is going to return to a populated earth He will have to return soon or some man or nation will try to destroy humankind. The threatened, or possible, nuclear holocaust, that is conceivable in our generation, points to a soon coming of Christ before such an event occurs.

Worldwide Gospel Preaching by the Year 2000

One of our Lord's well-known promises about the end of the age is found in Matthew 24:14, "And this gospel of the kingdom will be preached in all the world as a witness to all the nations, and then the end will come." Most prophecy scholars locate this worldwide preaching of the gospel during the Tribulation period. It is assumed this will be done under the ministry of the 144,000, in Revelation 7, who reach a "multitude that no man can number from every tongue, tribe and nation" (v.9). That means it will be fulfilled *after the rapture* of the church.

The point is, we are coming close to preaching the gospel to all the world in the very near future! At the 1992 National Convention of Religious Broadcasters, the heads of three worldwide Christian shortwave radio ministries shared their current decade evangelistic strategy. The presidents of Far Eastern Broadcasting ministries, HCJB in Quito, Equador, and Trans-World Radio, which covers Europe, have launched a plan to take the gospel via shortwave radio to the entire world "by the year 2000"! They represent the three largest radio networks in the world. My friend Bill Bright, whose vision has stirred my heart for over 40 years, announced that Campus Crusade For Christ International has a plan to "help reach the world for Christ by the year 2000." Other mission agencies have similar target dates.

While we know this prophecy will be fulfilled during the Tribulation, the fact that so many effective groups are working for the same target date, at a time when such an effort is technologically possible, does indeed suggest the coming of Christ for His church may soon be at hand. Also, there is the movings of the Holy Spirit throughout the world. As I read the *International World Religion Report,* which comes to my desk twice a month, I am amazed at the moving of the Holy Spirit in leading millions of souls to the Savior—all over the world. Since the fall of the Soviet Union, just a few years ago, God is opening many doors for gospel preaching which have been closed for over 70 years. Consequently, we hear of millions of people making decisions for Christ. South America too has seen millions of its people come to faith in Christ.

During the Reagan years, when communists tried to overpower

the young democracies of Central America, all five countries elected conservative presidents who were either professing Christians or favorable to Christianity. On one of my visits to his country, one of those presidents said to me that it was "the evangelicals that got me elected." The number of Christians had grown fourfold in his country, and it is they who went to the polls and elected him over his communist opponent. The same is true of the other countries. It can be accurately said that the amazing soul harvest in Central and South America in the last two decades is what saved those regions from going communist. Similar soul harvests are reported throughout the world, from Africa to China.

It is safe to say that Matthew 24:14 will soon be fulfilled, which means, the coming of Christ could be at hand.

The New World Order

One of the signs of the end is that the governments of the world will relinquish their sovereignty to one federal head, to become the international world leader of the future. Unknown to many in the world, there are already secret societies and organizations working timelessly to make that come to pass soon. During the past few years, shocking revelations have confirmed that, indeed, for over 200 years, many influential leaders of some of the most powerful countries of the world are committed to ushering in the one-world government.

So much has been said about secret orders like the Illuminati, founded in 1776, the Skull and Bones of Yale, founded in 1856, the Order at Oxford in 1904, the Club of Rome, the Fabian Society, the Bildeburgers. Others, are not secret, like the influential Council on Foreign Relations, founded in 1921, which established the Trilateral Commission in 1973. What is important about these organizations is that whenever their membership comes to light it includes the elitists who control government, banking, education, and media in their countries. Few Christians are ever found in such groups which often reveal a hostility to our Judeo-Christian culture and values.

Another thing these groups have in common, is that they are all working in one way or another for a world government. Some think it is Satanically inspired. Even if that can't be proven, the point is, when Satan does prepare the world for uniting under one master controller, he will probably use a system of interlocking secret organizations that seek to control the economy, the religion, and the media of the world. With this power he will be able to control the most powerful world governmental leaders.

NAFTA and the GATT world trade treaties, passed recently, are the result of such organizations, who believe they must unite the world commercially to make them so interdependent that they can merge the world into one constitution, judicial system, and government. Already plans have been made to divide the world into three currencies, the Japanese yen for the Orient, the German mark for Europe, and the U.S. dollar for the Americas. This is to be the first step toward a one-world currency—controlled by one panel or one person. A somewhat recent suggestion by one of the most powerful elite insiders, who controls several of these groups, is that they divide the world into ten regions, appoint a ruler over each, with a seat on the ruling council of the world (the expanded UN security council?). Who can say that the world is not already on the fast track toward a one-world government, which could be consummated in this or the next generation?

The Mark of the Beast—Technology Already Here

One of the best known prophecies of the Tribulation is that the "beast" or world leader popularly called the Antichrist, will have the ability to put his mark, "666," on the forehead and hand of the people. To buy or sell during that period, you will need that mark. For the first time in 2000 years, it is now technologically possible to enforce such a system. Micro-chips have already been invented that can be placed in the fatty tissue behind the ear, or in other places of the body, which could provide computer tracking. We are all familiar with the scanner at the check-out counter of most stores. All it would take is a computer program that required the "666" number on peoples' accounts, or hands, in order for them to "buy or sell." Mark of the beast technology is already here!

Revelation-Type Plagues Already Exist

One of the frightening events of the Tribulation period is the many plagues that will strike the people, in God's attempt to get them to repent of their sins and turn to Him. The two witnesses have the power to put plagues on their enemies, at the same time that the plagues of the trumpet and vial judgments occur. Although we do not know the extent of those plagues, we do know that the people who contract them will suffer so unbearably that they will begin to die.

Even without knowing the medical details of these plagues, we can already identify AIDS and STDS, or Sexually Transmitted Diseases, having similar types of effects on people. Four decades ago, the medical profession thought it had eliminated sexually transmitted diseases. Unfortunately they have returned with a vengeance. Penicillin and antibiotics worked for a while, but the diseases developed stronger strains, too powerful for drugs to contain, and today they are worse than before.

AIDS is one of the most frightening diseases of our times, particularly for the sexually promiscuous. Once it is contracted it is fatal. It spreads like wildfire and no cure seems to be on the horizon. In 1981, the United States reported its first case. Since then cases have reached into the millions. Experts predict it will infect ten million people by the year 2000, and that is probably underestimated. AIDS in Africa, the most tragically hit by AIDS, will soon reach 50 percent of the population, unless a cure is found. I am not saying AIDS is the fulfillment of Revelation, just that we already have that type of plague on our hands, and the most advanced scientific laboratories of our day can do nothing to halt it.

It is instructive that these diseases have hit in the last decade, along with the many other events typical of the last days.

Unprecedented Earthquakes and Natural Disasters

An increase in earthquakes, even multiple and enormous earthquakes was predicted by both our Lord in Matthew 24:7, and also by the apostle John in the book of Revelation, for the time of the end. Because of their frightening and uncontrolled intensity, earthquakes have always been considered a sign of God's judgment, at least since His destruction of Sodom and Gomorrah because of their sinful lifestyle.

For our purposes, I wish to call attention to the fact that something unusual is going on in nature during the 1990s. Some of the most disastrous "natural" catastrophes have occurred in both intensity and numbers. For example, killer earthquakes were very rare for centuries, numbering perhaps one each decade. Notice in the following chart how they have increased during the past five decades, according to the U.S. Geological Society:

- 1940–1949:   4
- 1950–1959:   9
- 1960–1969:   13
- 1970–1979:   56
- 1980–1989:   74

What has seismologists concerned is the obvious increase in killer earthquakes during the last five decades. Each decade has seen an increased number of earthquakes over the decade before it. The period between 1990–94 has already exceeded the number of killer quakes in the decade before it. The 7.2 quake in Kobe, Japan, which destroyed over 5000 lives and injured tens of thousands. This is thought to be the worst earthquake to hit Japan in almost 50 years. There have been frightening quakes in Africa, Ethiopia, Pakistan, Tibet, the Philippines, and of course San Francisco and Los Angeles, which toppled freeway bridges, leaving at least 57 dead. It is obvious that earthquakes are increasing with each passing decade. Something unusual is transpiring with planet Earth!

One seismologist at the Scripps Research Center in La Jolla, California, said, "It is almost as though the earth's plates are gyrating in anticipation of the world's greatest earthquake." Whether that is the one described in Revelation 6, 11, or 18, is yet to be determined. But who can doubt that we are seeing the very fulfillment of earthquake phenomenon that could be preparing the earth for the coming judgments of God as foretold for the Tribulation?

In 1993, a news report indicated there were other worldwide problems of nature:

- South Africa experienced widespread crop failures... floods...

- Bangladesh—nearly half under water, 316 people killed, 6 million homeless...
- 2100 people die in flooding in Southeast Asia...
- 1100 flood victims in Himalayan kingdom of Nepal...
- 700 die in floods in India...

In our own country, in one year we experienced hurricane Andrew in Florida, which destroyed 40,000 homes at a cost of over $20 billion. Fifty inches of snow paralyzed the East, causing Washington D.C. to close down. Floods hit the Mississippi valley at a cost of $20 billion. Early in 1995, torrential rains hit northern California and devastated a whole region. But it is not limited to America. Hailstones the size of tennis balls bombarded France, and torrential rains created what they called a "black rainstorm alert" in Hong Kong.

The proportions of these unnatural phenomenon can be seen in the fact that one of the world's oldest and most stable insurance companies, Lloyds of London, has had to pay so many claims of late it is on the verge of bankruptcy.

All this, and more is expected, at a time when all these other events indicate Christians today have very good reason to believe their Lord could come soon, to take them to their Father's house. Yet there is more.

The Potential Collapse of Russia

For centuries prophetic scholars have been convinced that "Rosh and the Chief prince of Rosh" mean that Russia and those who control will lead the march of the Arab world down to the mountains of Israel, where God will show Himself powerful to all the world by destroying their armies according to Ezekiel 38–39. Not only the etymology of the names leads us to identify this chief antagonist as Russia, but her location in "the uttermost part of the North," clearly means Russia, which is located north of Israel (38:6).

The problem is, for the past five years, ever since the fall of the Berlin Wall and the breakup of the old Soviet Union, the nation of Russia has been on shaky ground. First, their leader was the charismatic Boris Yeltsin, but his vice of alcoholism has all but rendered him ineffective. The economy of the country is in shambles as they refused to adopt full scale free enterprise but retained enough of the socialist policies that have stultified the economy. The country is in worse shape today than when it enjoyed freedom for the first time in 70 years. The unstable government makes it vulnerable to a takeover by the hard-line communists, who are just waiting in the wings to be brought back into control.

At risk is the peace of the world, because Russia and her independent satellite countries still have over 30,000 nuclear missiles pointed at the West. And one important factor should be remembered, Russia still maintains a close relationship with the Arab world. Actually, 55 million of her 250 million people are Arabs, plus their allies in the Middle East, all of whom hate Israel.

My point is, Russia is in precarious straits. She could have a revolution, become a dictatorship, or just collapse under her own bureaucratic weight and become a fifth-rate power. Her army is really not the fearful monster it was once pictured to be, since it is obvious she failed miserably in Afghanistan, and proved to be a paper tiger in her takeover of the little independent country of Chechnya.

It does not seem that time is on Russia's side. If she is going to be the major power that Ezekiel forecasts her to be, she had better make her move soon, or she won't be able to. Which means, if Russia is to go down against Israel, she had better do it soon!

This Generation Has the Capability of Fulfilling the Amazing Feat of Revelation 11:9

During the first three-and-a-half years of the Tribulation, the two supernatural witnesses, probably Moses and Elijah, will return to assist the children of Israel against their enemies. They will have power to "shut heaven so that no rain falls." They preach for 1260 days, and they have power over waters to "turn them to blood, and to strike the earth with all plagues" (v.6). When they finish their testimony they are so hated that people kill them and leave their bodies lying in the street for three days. Verse 9 says, "Those from the peoples, tribes, tongues, and nations (a description of the whole world) will see their dead bodies three and a half days."

Technologically, this has never been possible before. Today, however, people with televisions see bodies lying in the streets on the evening news. Just a decade ago that would have been impossible. But when the U.S. troops went into Panama in 1989, it was seen in 55 countries of the world. The expulsion of Iraq from Kuwait and the bombing of Israel during the Gulf War was seen nightly in 109 countries. By 1993, CNN claimed to be in over 200 countries of the world daily, and still growing.

This is the first generation to see the possible fulfillment of that end-time prophecy.

The Year-Day Theory of the Jews and Early Christians

The oldest theory about when Christ would come back to this earth was taught by some rabbis even before Jesus' birth. Since they accepted the Old Testament, many of the early Christians also espoused it. Basically, they believed that since the Lord created the earth, sun, moon, stars, and man in six days, and then rested for a day, and since one day is as "a thousand years," as God reckons time, then Christ will come back around the year 2000. They teach that since there were about 4000 years prior to Christ and about 2000 since his birth, what better fulfillment of the "day of rest" (or 1000 years) than His glorious coming back to earth to set up 1000 years of millennial "rest," when the world will experience peace, and blessing, without war.

Now I am not suggesting that we adopt the theory. I do not find it specifically taught in Scripture. I only suggest it here because it is the oldest of theories, and if true, it would culminate in our generation. The exact number of years from Adam to the death of Christ may be off by several years. So, too, the actual dating system since Christ's death and resurrection, which was not assigned until at least six centuries after the fact. Consequently, the actual date of the year 2000 may be off 4 to 40 years or more.

The point is not that the year 2000 is the year. I doubt that it is. The point is, it is well within the "season," or generation. Our generation.

Jesus Christ may not come in this generation, no one really knows! Of that we can be definite! However, our generation has more reason to believe His coming *could* be during our lifetime than any other generation before us. For that reason we should "number our days" and live each one in the light that He may come at any time.

Don't Forget to Subtract Seven Years

If you are tempted to use this theory of the early church, remember that that is all it is—theory. Do not forget, we have been talking about Jesus' glorious appearing. There are no signs for the rapture. All signs of the Lord's return relate to His glorious appearing. Therefore, you must subtract at least the seven-year Tribulation period when thinking about the rapture. Consequently, don't be surprised if you realize it is later than you think! Christ could indeed come today, or tomorrow, or soon.

The big question is, are you ready? If you have never repented of your sins and by faith in Jesus' resurrection invited Him into your heart, please do so immediately. It would be tragic to know what you do and yet be like 61 percent of the American population who indicated to the 1994 *U.S. News and World Report* pollsters that they believed Christ will return to this earth—but that they are not ready for Him. (Only 38 percent of the population profess a "born again" experience.) May I suggest that if you have any doubt, that you invite Jesus Christ into your heart. Consider saying a prayer similar to the following:

> Dear God:
> I am a sinner! I believe Jesus Christ died on the cross for my sins and rose the third day. I wish to repent of my sins and do confess them to you, and to ask that you forgive me and save me. I give myself completely to you. Amen.

If that is your need, make it your sincere prayer and trust God for your salvation. Believe the Scripture that says, "Whosoever shall call on the Name of the Lord shall be saved" (Romans 10:13).

If you are already a Christian, let me ask you a question: Are you ready for Jesus' return? Oh, I know you will be raptured when He comes, but are you living the kind of life you want Him to find you living when He comes? Are you faithfully serving Him? Are you a regular part of a Bible-believing church? If not, resurrender your life to Him, live pleasing to Him, and do whatever He leads you to do.

Our Lord's final statement in Revelation is still appropriate. "'And behold, I am coming quickly, and My reward is with Me, to give to each one according to his work. I am the Alpha and the Omega, the Beginning and the End, the First and the Last.' Blessed are those who do His commandments, that they may have the right to the tree of life, and may enter in through the gates into the city."

THE PRIORITIES
IN LIGHT OF
HIS COMING

CHARLES R. SWINDOLL

Charles R. Swindoll, D.D.
President, Dallas Theological Seminary
President, Insight for Living radio ministry
Author of nine Gold Medallion books

In the first chapter, we investigated the scriptural evidence of Christ's return...not in great detail, but sufficiently to realize that He is indeed coming back. We cannot ignore the fact that, while His return is sure, He may not return in this generation—or even the next. So what do we do in the meantime? That question may not be a major doctrine but it certainly is a major issue. The late Francis Schaeffer asked the right question, "How Should We Then Live?" What ought to occupy our time? What do we do between now and when He returns?

There once lived a farmer named William Miller. It was back in the nineteenth century. Miller began a religion. One of the marks of his religion was an intense belief in Christ's return. He was notorious for setting dates. He and his followers (known as the Millerites) often met for camp meetings. During one of these meetings, a date was set for the Lord's return. The Millerites decided to pull together and rally around the prediction regardless of public reaction.

The date was announced: Jesus would return between March 21, 1842, and March 21, 1843. During that year they were to ready themselves for Christ's arrival. He was sure to return! To make a year-long story short, He didn't. Disappointment swept through the Millerite ranks, though Miller himself was undaunted. He had simply "miscalculated." So he sharpened his pencil, refigured the details, and set another date. This time Jesus would *definitely* return. The announcement was made on August 12, 1844: He would come between October 20 and October 22, 1844. "Get ready for the end of the world."

As time drew very near, a sign was displayed on a Philadelphia store window:

THIS SHOP WILL BE CLOSED IN HONOR OF THE KING OF KINGS WHO WILL APPEAR ABOUT THE TWENTIETH OF OCTOBER. GET READY, FRIENDS, TO CROWN HIM LORD OF ALL.

A group of about two hundred Millerites sold or gave away their possessions (I've often wondered why they sold their things if they were sure the world was going to end) and prepared their wardrobe for the soon-coming King. They gathered and waited in white robes for His coming. And waited. And waited. And waited. October 20 came and went. So did the 21st and the 22nd, and, of course, the 23rd.... Five years later, William Miller died. I think the wisest statement that was ever made by the Millerites was put on his tombstone. It reads, "At the appointed time the end shall be." Finally, they demonstrated good theology! Not on March 21,

1842, or on October 20, 1844. Not on July 7, 1909, or on November 25, 1947, nor even the first day of the year 2000, but *at the appointed time* the end shall be.

It may not be when you think it's going to be. It may not even be as soon as you think it will be. Chances are good it will be sooner than many anticipate. But, again I repeat, no one can say when. To put it bluntly, date-setters are out to lunch. Always have been... always will be! No one knows for sure. But there are a couple of things we *do* know. We can be sure of both.

Historically

We are sure that Christ will return. As we saw in the previous chapter, that fact is well-documented. Look at Matthew, chapter 24, for example...

> Heaven and earth will pass away, but My words shall not pass away. But of that day and hour no one knows, not even the angels of heaven, nor the Son, but the Father alone. For the coming of the Son of Man will be just like the days of Noah. For as in those days which were before the flood they were eating and drinking, they were marrying and giving in marriage (vv. 35–38a).

The picture Jesus is painting is a normal lifestyle. Before the flood in Noah's day, some people were working, others were sleeping. Some were being born, while others were marrying. People were dying. It was a normal, everyday lifestyle.

> ... until the day that Noah entered the ark, and they did not understand until the flood came and took them all

away, so shall the coming of the Son of Man be. Then there shall be two men in the field; one will be taken, and one will be left. Two women will be grinding at the mill; one will be taken, and one will be left. Therefore be on the alert, for you do not know which day your Lord is coming (vv. 38b–42).

Now the point here is rather obvious. We do not know the exact time, but we are absolutely sure of the fact. He *is* coming again. It will occur when life on earth is rolling along.

Now before we consider the second thing we know for sure, let's listen to the words of a reputable student of prophecy:

A short time ago, I took occasion to go through the New Testament to mark each reference to the coming of the Lord Jesus Christ and to observe the use made of that teaching about His coming. I was struck anew with the fact that almost without exception, when the coming of Christ is mentioned in the New Testament, it is followed by an exhortation to godliness and holy living. While the study of prophecy will give us proof of the authority of the Word of God, will reveal the purpose of God and the power of God, and will give us the peace and assurance of God, we have missed the whole purpose of the study of prophecy if it does not conform us to the Lord Jesus Christ in our daily living.[1]

You see, God never intended the truth of His Son's return simply to stir up our curiosity or to give us the big-time tingles. God has given us the truth concerning His Son's return to prompt holy living. We study the prophetic word so we can keep our act cleaned up, so that we will be ready at any moment and will not be embarrassed to meet Him face to face. You may remember that on the heels of that great New Testament chapter on resurrection and Jesus' return, 1 Corinthians 15, the final verse exhorts us to stay at the tasks of responsible living.

> Therefore, my dear brothers, stand firm. Let nothing move you. Always give yourselves fully to the work of the Lord, because you know that your labor in the Lord is not in vain (v. 58, niv).

Prophetically

We also know this: Nothing stands in the way of Christ's return. That is why I have repeatedly used the term *imminent*...Jesus' coming could occur at any moment. In other words, there is no future event in God's timetable that must take place before Christ comes in the clouds for His own. Nothing! Candidly, I find that rather exciting. Since we know for sure He's coming, yet we don't know for sure when...any day or any hour could be the one!

H. L. Turner was right, over a hundred years ago, when he wrote:

> It may be at morn, when the day is awakening,
> When sunlight through darkness and shadow is break-
> ing,
> That Jesus will come in the fullness of glory,
> To receive from the world His own.
>
> O joy! O delight! Should we go without dying,
> No sickness, no sadness, no dread and no crying,

Caught up through the clouds with our Lord into glory,
When Jesus receives His own.[2]

My maternal grandfather, whom I loved dearly, used to say that he looked forward to dying because he wanted to go through the whole process as a Christian. Rather than bypassing death, he wanted to go through it. He wanted to know in a conscious manner, the joy of life beyond the grave. He wanted to experience his body's bursting out of the ground, glorified and fitted for eternity, brought immediately into the Lord's presence. As I recall, he used to say that those who were going to be taken up while they are alive are only getting part of the blessing. But those who go through the whole death process "are going to get their money's worth!" In fact, they get preferential treatment. As we saw earlier, we will not precede those who have fallen asleep. They will be raised first, and then we will be brought up with them, glorified, to meet the Lord in the air.

Well, dear, old L. O. Lundy got his wish. He has died and his body awaits the Savior's arrival. Any day now he's going to get his "money's worth."

What if He doesn't return in this generation? What if that little family you're beginning to raise grows up and you grow old, still waiting for the Lord's return? What if you become a grandparent or a great-grandparent in the distant years of the future, and He still hasn't come back? How are we to conduct ourselves? What does the Bible teach about life during the interlude?

But...In the Meantime

There are four words I want you to remember. You might even want to commit them to memory. These four words represent

God's "marching orders" for us—our in-the-meantime standard operating procedure:

- Occupy
- Purify
- Watch
- Worship

If someone asks you, "What are we supposed to do before Christ comes? What is our involvement? Our commitment?" These four words will provide an answer. They are not only wise words of practical counsel, all four are taught in the Scripture. Let's examine each one in greater detail.

Occupy

Dr. Luke records a parable Jesus taught in which He addressed the importance of life continuing on until the Lord returns. Take the time to read the entire account.

> And while they were listening to these things, He went on to tell a parable, because He was near Jerusalem, and they supposed that the kingdom of God was going to appear immediately. He said therefore, "A certain nobleman went to a distant country to receive a kingdom for himself, and then return. And he called ten of his slaves, and gave them ten minas, and said to them, "Do business with this until I come back." But his citizens hated him, and sent a delegation after him, saying, "We do not want this man to reign over us." And it came about that when he returned, after receiving the kingdom, he ordered that these slaves, to whom he had given the money, be called to him in order that he might know what business they

had done. And the first appeared, saying, "Master, your mina has made ten minas more." And he said to him, "Well done, good slave, because you have been faithful in a very little thing, be in authority over ten cities." And the second came, saying, "Your mina, master, has made five minas." And he said to him also, "And you are to be over five cities." And another came, saying, "Master, behold your mina, which I kept put away in a handkerchief; for I was afraid of you, because you are an exacting man; you take up what you did not lay down, and reap what you did not sow." He said to him, "By your own words I will judge you, you worthless slave. Did you know that I am an exacting man, taking up what I did not lay down, and reaping what I did not sow? Then why did you not put the money in the bank, and having come, I would have collected it with interest?" And he said to the bystanders, "Take the mina away from him, and give it to the one who has the ten minas." And they said to him, "Master, he has ten minas already." "I tell you, that to everyone who has shall more be given, but from the one who does not have, even what he does have shall be taken away. But these enemies of mine, who did not want me to reign over them, bring them here, and slay them in my presence" (Luke 19:11–27).

A "mina" was a lot of money, in fact about a hundred day's wages (nearly twenty dollars in those days). The nobleman gave his slaves ten of those coins as he instructed all of them to "do business" while he was away.

You may wish to circle the words "do business." More than

one version of Scripture renders the same command "occupy." "Do business," however, is a good way of saying it. The point is clear. It was the nobleman's desire that his servants not sit back, doing nothing—letting his money collect dust—until he returned. But they failed to do as He had commanded.

Finally, he returned. Immediately the nobleman was interested in their activity while he had been away. The report was anything but pleasing. Except for the first one who had multiplied his investment tenfold and the second one fivefold, the slaves had failed to "occupy" during his absence.

The lessons from this story are numerous, but it is noteworthy that the nobleman (Jesus) smiled upon the wise use of money during the interlude. He was pleased with the investments of those who made much of the goods of this earth. That's a part of doing business. To put it in different words, we "occupy" when we live responsibly, work diligently, plan wisely, think realistically, invest carefully. In neither the Old nor New Testament is laziness smiled upon, especially laziness that is rationalized because one believes in the soon-coming of Christ. Our Lord frowns on the lack of discipline and diligence. He smiles on a well-ordered private life. He is pleased with the wise use of our time and proper handling of our possessions. Some excuse irresponsibility by giving it a spiritual-sounding title, like "walking by faith" or "trusting the Lord." Let's not tempt the Lord with such rationalization.

There once lived a group of Christians who bought into that mentality. They thought that since they knew Christ was coming and since their teacher, the apostle Paul himself, had assured them that the Lord was coming soon, why work? Why even concern themselves with the mundane details of everyday life? They'd just spend their days awaiting His coming. And until He arrived they would live off of others. If others chose to work, fine; but they would be the ones who "lived by faith." Once Paul heard of that, he jumped on it like a hen on a June bug:

> Now we command you, brethren, in the name of our Lord Jesus Christ, that you keep aloof from every brother who leads an unruly life and not according to the tradition which you received from us. For you yourselves know how you ought to follow our example, because we did not act in an undisciplined manner among you, nor did we eat anyone's bread without paying for it, but with labor and hardship we kept working night and day so that we might not be a burden to any of you; not because we do not have the right to this, but in order to offer ourselves as a model for you, that you might follow our example. For even when we were with you, we used to give you this order: If anyone will not work, neither let him eat. For we hear that some among you are leading an undisciplined life, doing no work at all, but acting like busybodies (2 Thessalonians 3:6–12).

Honestly, doesn't a part of that sound like your dad's counsel? I can just hear my father's voice in those words! Especially, "If anyone will not work, neither let him eat." But this is more than a father's advice…these are words from the authoritative Scripture. Those who have a right to eat are those who work. Even though we believe strongly in Christ's soon return, and even though we claim to be walking by faith, if we plan to eat while waiting, working is God's plan for us.

Then this final admonition:

But as for you, brethren, do not grow weary of doing good. And if anyone does not obey our instruction in this letter, take special note of that man and do not associate with him, so that he may be put to shame (vv. 13–14).

I call that straight talk—hard talk.

Every once in a while we meet up with some dear soul with eyes at half-mast, who wants to sit on a hill, strum a guitar, eat birdseed, and sing Christian folk tunes. His (or her) idea of faith-life is just gathering dew and watching the weeds and daisies grow up all around. This Scripture strikes at the heart of such thinking. God has limited patience with people who irresponsibly hide behind "faith" as they leave it to others to pay their bills.

And to make matters worse, they say the reason they're doing that is because they *really* love the Lord Jesus. No, more often than not the reason they do that is because they are lazy. For them, the soon-coming of Christ is a wonderful cop-out. The next time one of them attempts to quote verses to support their rationalization, I suggest you counter with 2 Thessalonians 3:10—"If anyone will not work, neither let him eat." There are still a few Christians who think manual labor is president of Mexico.

So much for "occupy." Get a job. Work hard. Think realistically. Plan ahead. Reorder your private world. Get your act together. Live responsibly. Invest carefully.

Our Lord expects nothing less.

Purify

There is a second word to remember while we're in the process of preparing for his coming, *purify*. I find biblical support for this in Titus 2:11–14:

For the grace of God has appeared, bringing salvation to all men, instructing us to deny ungodliness and worldly desires and to live sensibly, righteously and godly in the present age, looking for the blessed hope and the appearing of the glory of our great God and Savior, Christ Jesus; who gave Himself for us, that He might redeem us from every lawless deed and purify for Himself a people for His own possession, zealous for good deeds.

Let me interject a telltale sign of heresy: a ministry that emphasizes the Lord's return but does not, with equal gusto, emphasize a godly life. Mark it down. Whoever highlights the coming of Christ is also responsible to teach the importance of a pure life. Why not? They mesh together, like teeth in gears. If indeed He is coming again, there is one thing we want to have in place—personal purity.

I wouldn't have much confidence in a person who prides himself in being a good surgeon who at the same time doesn't worry too much about sterile instruments. Wonder how many patients he would have if he said, "To tell you the truth, I've got a new plan in surgery. We do all of our surgery in the back room here at the clinic. I just push this stuff out of the way, then you crawl up on the table and I'll give you a shot. You've got nothing to worry about."

One thing about practicing good medicine is that you cooperate with the rules of sterilization. You can't be too careful about cleanliness and sterility. And if anyone is going to talk about the coming of the Lord Jesus, then be sure that the same person balances all that talk with an emphasis on purity of life.

The apostle John agrees wholeheartedly with the apostle Paul's words to Titus:

See how great a love the Father has bestowed upon us, that we should be called children of God; and such we are. For this reason the world does not know us, because it did not know Him. Beloved, now we are children of God, and it has not appeared as yet what we shall be. We know that, when He appears, we shall be like Him, because we shall see Him just as He is. And every one who has this hope fixed on Him purifies himself, just as He is pure (1 John 3:1–3).

Why, of course!

We have been to enough splendid, unforgettable weddings to realize that the object of attention is the beautiful bride, dressed in white. The excitement of the entire ceremony occurs when the center aisle doors are opened and the organist begins to play full crescendo, as the bride, with her proud (and often frightened) father are making their way down to the alter.

Finally, she stands there in all her purity. Although I have officiated at hundreds of wedding ceremonies, I will never get over the thrill of that moment! Did you know that our Lord often calls His church His bride? Like a bride of beauty and purity in no other color than white, all Christians represent that they are pure "spiritual" virgins awaiting the joys and intimacies of heavenly marriage with their Groom. What an analogy! John's words seem so appropriate: "Everyone who has this hope...purifies himself."

But how? How can we maintain such a commitment to purity? We learn to live by short accounts. We refuse to let the filth of our life stack up. We don't ignore even the little things that have broken our fellowship with God or with others. We are to live, in the words of the New Testament, with "a conscience void of offense." That's how we can dress in white for His coming, as a bride prepares for her groom. Perhaps all of that is included in our judging ourselves so that we may not be judged.

Watch

Let's look next at the word *watch*. In the Gospel by Mark, chapter 13, the word *watch* is implied in the commands "Keep on the alert!" and "Stay on the alert!" and "Be on the alert!" Observe those three commands in these seven verses:

> Heaven and earth will pass away, but My words will not pass away. But of that day or hour no one knows, not even the angels in heaven, nor the Son, but the Father alone. Take heed, *keep on the alert;* for you do not know when the appointed time is. It is like a man, away on a journey, who upon leaving his house and putting his slaves in charge, assigning to each one his task, also commanded the doorkeeper to *stay on the alert.* Therefore, *be on the alert*—for you do not know when the master of the house is coming, whether in the evening, at midnight, at cockcrowing, or in the morning—lest he come suddenly and find you asleep. And what I say to you I say to all, *"Be on the alert!"* (vv. 31–37 emphasis mine).

In light of the urgency in Jesus' words, I find it nothing short of remarkable how many days we live without a single conscious thought flashing through our minds regarding Christ's return…not even a passing thought. Isn't it amazing? I've noticed that those who become increasingly more sensitive to spiritual things fix more and more of their attention on His coming. And they don't need the reminder from others.

We have all had the same experience of someone's telling us that he's going to come see us on a particular day. He doesn't state a time, but he tells you it'll be sometime during that day. As time wears on through that day, the more often we look. We check the street out front so often that we get the drapes dirty! We're look-ing. We're watching. We keep waiting until night falls. We turn the front porch light on. We make sure the door is unlocked. We check it four more times to make sure! Why? Because we're anx-iously anticipating our friend's coming. We watch every set of headlights that comes around the corner. We stay alert. We are thinking about it. That's what our Lord has in mind here.

I'll be honest with you. Maintaining a balance in all this is tough to do. When I teach on prophetic subjects, I feel a little bit like a parent who warns a child against a stranger. Hoping to guard people from fanaticism, I might go too far and talk them out of being full of anticipation. Parents who teach children to be careful about strangers have to be careful not to overdo it. Because a child can begin to live so suspiciously that everyone is in ques-tion—no one can be trusted. It's easy for a child to "overlearn" such warnings.

So while I warn you against the extreme of foolish fanaticism, let me quickly add that God honors watching, having a heart that pumps faster, when we think of His Son's return. In fact, do you know that there's a reward promised? There's an actual crown that will be given for people who live lives full of anticipation of His coming.

I have fought the good fight, I have finished the course, I have kept the faith; in the future there is laid up for me the crown of righteousness, which the Lord, the righteous Judge, will award to me on that day; and not only to me, but also to all who have loved His appearing (2 Timothy 4:7–8).

The "crown of righteousness" is reserved for all who live their lives anticipating the Savior's return. He honors us for living with a watchful eye. By the way, it's a whole lot easier to keep our lives pure when we realize His coming is near. There's a lot of built-in motivation when we think that His return will usher in the "Judgment Seat of Christ." That is why Jesus exhorts us:

Be dressed in readiness, and keep your lamps alight…And be sure of this, that if the head of the house had known at what hour the thief was coming, he would not have allowed his house to be broken into. You too, be ready; for the Son of Man is coming at an hour that you do not expect (Luke 12:35, 39–40).

Worship

In all my years of attending church services and hearing the Bible taught, I cannot remember hearing much said about the importance of worship as we await Christ's coming. But it is clearly an emphasis in Scripture, just as important as occupying, purifying, and watching.

The biblical basis for my comments on worship is found in 1 Corinthians 11:23–26.

For I received from the Lord that which I also delivered to you, that the Lord Jesus in the night in which He was betrayed took bread; and when He had given thanks, He broke it, and said, "This is My body, which is for you; do this in remembrance of Me." In the same way He took the cup also, after supper, saying, "This cup is the new covenant in My blood; do this, as often as you drink it, in remembrance of Me." For as often as you eat this bread and drink the cup, you proclaim the Lord's death until He comes.

How long are Christians to participate in worship? How long are we to gather around the Lord's Table and hold in our hands the elements that symbolize our Savior's body and blood? He tells us in the last three words—"until He comes." Every time we worship around the Lord's Table, it is another reminder that He's coming. One of these times will be our last time to observe it on earth. It's kind of exciting, isn't it? It will be our last spiritual meal on earth together. But until then, we are to worship the Lord Christ. Every meal at His table is another reminder that His coming is nearer. We worship Him with great anticipation.

How to Stay Alert and Ready

There's no reason to get complicated about this matter of in-the-meantime living. A couple of thoughts seem worth emphasizing.

The first is: *Remember Jesus promised it would occur someday* (and He tells the truth!). Keep that in mind. When you read the paper, think of His coming. And remember His promise to return as you see events transpiring that relate to the nation Israel or relate to calamities in our times or those signs and tragedies He predicted would be telltale signs of His arrival. Each of these events—while not directly connected to Christ's return—collectively assure us that we are certainly living in the last days. Call it to mind when you hear of such events, when you lose a loved one, or when something of value is cut out from under you. Hope in the future takes the sting out of the present. Life won't be so hard if we learn to live in the conscious hope of His soon return.

Here's a second tip: *Realize the promise could occur today* (and that will be the moment of truth). Let me make a suggestion. Let me help you form a new habit for getting out of bed in the morning. Just as soon as your tootsies hit the floor, even before you lift yourself up to your feet headed for the day, look out the window. As you look, repeat these two lines:

> "Good morning, Lord."
> "Will I see you today?"

I've started doing that and it is amazing how often I have seen Him in my morning or in the face of a child, in a circumstance that I would otherwise have missed Him, in a response from an individual, in an interruption, in a telephone conversation. One of these days, sooner than many of us think, we'll see Him in death. And who knows? One of those days in which we've said those two sentences will be the day He'll come. How great to be able to say "Why, hello, Lord…I've been looking for you."

When former President Eisenhower was vacationing in Denver a number of years ago, his attention was called to an open letter in a local newspaper, which told how six-year-old Paul Haley, dying of incurable cancer, had expressed a wish to see the President of the United States. Spontaneously, in one of those gracious gestures remembered long after a man's most carefully prepared speeches are forgotten, the President decided to grant the boy's request.

So one Sunday morning in August, a big limousine pulled up outside the Haley home and out stepped the President. He walked up to the door and knocked.

Mr. Donald Haley opened the door, wearing blue jeans, an old shirt, and a day's growth of beard. Behind him was his little son, Paul. Their amazement at finding President Eisenhower on their doorstep can be imagined.

"Paul," said the President to the little boy, "I understand you want to see me. Glad to see you." Then he shook hands with the six-year-old, and took him out to see the presidential limousine, shook hands again and left.

The Haleys and their neighbors, and a lot of other people, will probably talk about this kind and thoughtful deed of a busy President for a long time to come. Only one person was not entirely happy about it—that was Mr. Haley. He can never forget how he was dressed when he opened the door. "Those jeans, the old shirt, the unshaven face—what a way to meet the President of the United States," he said.[3]

I can tell you a situation that could be a lot more embarrassing than that. One day there will be a shout, a voice, a trumpet blast, and we won't even have *time* to change clothes. Instantly, we'll be swept into His glorious, eternal presence.

But...until He comes, what? Remember the watchwords: occupy, purify, watch, and worship. If you're engaged in those four things, you won't have to get ready, you'll *be* ready! No need to set a date or quite your job or dress in white. Just live every day as if this were the one.

"At the appointed time, the end shall be." One of these days will be "the appointed time." You are ready, aren't you?

1. J. Dwight Pentecost, *Prophecy for Today* (Grand Rapids: Zondervan, 1961), 10.
2. H. L. Turner, "It May Be at Morn."
3. Billy Graham, *World Aflame* (Garden City, N.Y.: Doubleday, 1965) 206–7.

FINAL THOUGHTS

Set Your Mind
on Heaven

JOSEPH M. STOWELL

Joseph M. Stowell
President of Moody Bible Institute
Author and popular conference speaker.

In 1988 a Bible teacher announced in his booklet entitled *Eighty-eight Reasons Why Christ Will Return in '88* that the second coming of Christ would occur that September. The book received much publicity and attracted a large following. His followers became passionate in their belief that Christ would be returning within the year. A video was released that dramatized the detailed proof of the prediction, and people sent me copies of the booklet and video, hoping as president of Moody that I would help warn the church.

I reviewed the booklet and did not believe the author accurately handled Scripture passages, particularly in light of the fact that Christ predicted that no man would know the time of His coming. Of course, September came and went without Christ's return. Among Christians, a few people were greatly disappointed, some were indifferent, and others felt embarrassed by the prophecy.

Still, my reaction—and that of many Christians—was an increased awareness that Christ could come back at any time. The implications sent my mind heavenward.

On the actual September morning that the author had pinpointed for the return of Christ, I rose from bed and for a moment wondered, *What if I am wrong and he is right? What if this is the day?* At the breakfast table, my family engaged in a lively discussion about it.

My daughter, Libby, walked down the driveway with me, continuing the discussion as I headed for my car to drive to my office. As I stepped into my car, Libby waved and said, "Hey, Dad…see ya in heaven."

My thoughts during that day were often of heaven.

Think of the difference it would make if each day heaven were so real to us that we anticipated being there by the day's end.

ETERNALLY DIFFERENT

For most of us, heaven is something that we have to intentionally set our minds on. It's worth it. The more we make heaven our preoccupation, the more our lives become radically transformed. People, possessions, career, time, pain, and pleasure all have meaning when viewed through the lens of heaven.

When our minds are set on heaven, a radical change occurs in our thoughts and attitudes. Hoping in heaven in the biblical sense is indeed transforming. As C. S. Lewis notes,

Hope is one of the Theological virtues. This means that a continual looking forward to the eternal world is not (as some modern people think) a form of escapism or wishful thinking, but one of the things a Christian is meant to do. It does not mean that we are to leave the present world as it is. If you read history you will find that the Christians who did most for the present world were just those who thought most of the next.[1]

The reality of eternity was the central motivation of the disciples during the early days of the church. The resurrection of Christ proved to them that heaven was real. Since there was life after death, nothing on this side could distract them. For them the other side was worth living for—and dying for if necessary. Nothing this passing world offered could deter them from living for eternity. Heaven was the primary reference point of their existence.

RIVETED TO HEAVEN

Making heaven our primary point of reference transforms us as well. What does it mean to make heaven our ultimate point of reference?

Points of reference rivet our attention and alter our behavior. When a college student prepares for a major grade-point-threatening test, he views all of life through the grid of that impending exam. If he neglects that point of reference—if he fails to prepare—he feels guilt and fear. If he gives proper attention to that point of reference, he will begin to do things he's never done before. He will say no to other less-important activities such as pick-up basketball and instead spend a long night at the library, sifting through his research notes and resources as though he were a scholar.

We all have points of reference. They dictate who we are, what we dream about, where we go, and what we do when we get there. Among these may be marriage, a vacation, a promotion, a baby soon to be born, a new home, a new car, retirement, a memory, an aged parent, ongoing sickness, or long-term sorrow.

Interestingly, life ultimately makes us somewhat cynical about our most anticipated points of reference since experiencing them is never quite as satisfying as we thought. Receiving an "A" on this exam soon becomes a distant memory with another exam to follow. We grow accustomed to a new house, and it's no longer new. A new car becomes used and out-of-date. Retirement becomes meaningless and depressing unless we discover new passions to spark our interest.

We experience a gnawing sense of incompleteness because we were built for something to look forward to, for something beyond ourselves, without which we are not whole. It is heaven for which we were built and redeemed. The disappointment we feel in earth-side experiences is an indication of heaven in our hearts.

Lewis again explains the issue well, writing:

> Most people, if they had really learned to look into their own hearts, would know that they do want, and want acutely, something that cannot be had in this world. There are all sorts of things in this world that offer to give it to you, but they never quite keep their promise.[2]

Heaven must become the target of our hearts. It's what we are meant to aim for.

An unalterable focus on heaven appears throughout Scripture. The first mention of heaven, though indirect, occurs in Genesis 3, when God promises Adam that one day his enemy would be defeated (verse 15). The first patriarch of Israel, Abraham, "was looking for the city which has foundations, whose architect and builder is God" (Hebrews 11:10). Other references are more direct. David looked forward to seeing his dead son again (2 Samuel 12:23), and the psalmist could cope with the prosperity of the wicked because he knew his God would ultimately receive him into paradise (Psalm 73).

In the teachings of Christ our gaze is lifted toward heaven. In the writings of Paul, Peter, James, and John we read about a certain, future home. In Revelation, John rivets our attention as God judges Satan, sin, and sinners; destroys this present world and all that is defiled by sin; and in a glorious conclusion introduces the new heaven and the new earth and establishes the City of God as the centerpiece.

Once we are convinced of this glorious consummation of sin-defiled time, space, and history and are introduced to eternity and its heaven, we are never the same again. When seen in its all-encompassing reality, heaven quickly becomes our all-consuming point of reference. It looms above everything else, trivializing that which is earthbound and lesser.

RADICALLY ALTERED

When we make heaven our reference point, we will know it because everything on this side becomes radically rearranged. At least seven aspects of our lives become wonderfully changed as a result of setting "your mind on things above" (Colossians 3:1–2).

Posture Toward God

First, *our posture toward God is radically changed.* We change from being temporalists—those consumed by the gain of the moment—to being eternalists—those consumed by the reality of God in eternity.

Remember the man who called to Christ from the crowd, "Tell my brother to divide the family inheritance with me" (Luke 12:13)? He had fixed his hope in life on the income from his inheritance, and his brother had not given him his share. Christ seized the moment and said, "Watch out! Be on your guard against all kinds of greed; a man's life does not consist in the abundance of his possessions" (verse 15).

Jesus then told the story of a man of great wealth (verses 16–21). To celebrate his success the man threw a party and invited all his friends to come. He commanded that they should eat, drink, and be merry. But, as Christ noted, a surprise guest came to the party: God. He said to the supposedly shrewd and successful man, "You fool!" He was a fool not because of all that stuff that he had in his barns, but because he was a *temporalist* rather than an *eternalist*. He had never thought of his life beyond this fleeting world. "This very night your life will be demanded from you. Then who will get what you have prepared for yourself?" (verse 20).

In this parable, Christ stretched this wealthy businessman's definition of life to include the reality of eternity, to the moment when he would present his soul to a holy God without the credentials of his earth-side success. That's a penetrating thought for all of us who have assumed that life derives value through an embossed title on a business card.

Millionaire Norman Miller, chairman of Interstate Batteries and a racing car enthusiast, has realized that, more than earthly success, he needs to be reconciled to the God of eternity through Christ. Having accepted Christ, he now runs his business with eternity's values in view. Norman sponsors a weekly Bible study held in the Dallas warehouse of Interstate Batteries, where drivers and salesmen also pray for a stronger commitment to Christ, their family, their country, and their job of selling automobile batteries.

Miller has made Interstate the leading replacement battery manufacturer in North America, with revenues of $350 million in 1994. And he is sold out to Christ. "I need to be faithful to Jesus 100 percent of the time," declares Miller. "And that includes my business."[3]

Perspective on Possessions

The second outcome of a life focused on heaven is a *proper attitude toward our possessions*. Christ indicates that fixing our hearts on heaven also will revise our perspective on our possessions.

The old bumper sticker is right: "You can't take it with you." It has been well said, "You won't find a funeral hearse pulling a U-Haul trailer." Heaven-convinced Christians regard everything they have on earth as an investment in heaven. Our possessions become not something to be stockpiled here, as symbols of our significance, but rather commodities to be used for eternal gain.

How do you view your time, talents, material goods, and finances? Are they commodities for your own consumption or capital that you can invest in eternal gain?

On October 27, 1993, a series of fires raged through parts of southern California, fanned by the notorious Santa Ana winds coming off the desert. One area hit especially hard was Laguna Hills, a beautiful upper-class community set inland from the Pacific Ocean. House after house was torched by the wind-swept blaze. Flames jumped from rooftop to rooftop, finding fuel in the cedar shake shingles.

After the fire swept through the neighborhood, only ash-covered foundations remained where scores of homes once stood. But there was one exception. The home of building contractor To Bui stood tall. The contractor wanted his home to last, so he had constructed the roof with concrete and tile. The fire tested the roof, found it inflammable, and skipped over it to others. In fact, newspapers across the country carried the dramatic photo of that one house standing amid acres of burned houses.

God's Word indicates that what we do here with all we possess will be evaluated at the bema seat of Christ. Like Bui, we want to be wise builders. We want to construct our lives out of materials that will stand the testing by the fires of judgment. When we enter His presence, the blaze of His glory will burn away everything that is not fit for eternity. Those activities and possessions won't necessarily be bad, just that which was merely earthbound in its nature. The only things of value, the only things that will remain, will be what we have done on this side that make a difference in the world to come.

Paul says our earth-side activities and resources that have been used for eternal gain will endure as though they were gold, silver, or precious stones. All other things will burn as if they were wood, hay, or straw (see 1 Corinthians 3:11–14).

When we do not invest our possessions in eternal gain, we become what Francis Schaeffer called "ash-heap Christians." Such Christians don't necessarily live evil lives, but their stay on earth simply has no effect on eternity. Schaeffer noted that there will be many standing before Christ at the bema seat "knee deep in ashes with hands empty" of anything solid and worthwhile to bring to the Savior on that day.[4]

What earthly possessions do we have that can be used for

gain in the world to come?

Let's begin with the people in our lives—our family and friends. Are we willing to give ourselves and those we love to honoring God *now* and telling others about the Redeemer *now?*

Edward, a student from the Ukraine, is studying at Moody Bible Institute so that he might go back and train other pastors and leaders in that needy land. As sometimes happens on college campuses, he has fallen hopelessly in love with a fellow student, Linda. She enrolled at Moody with a heart committed to serve God wherever He led her. She probably would have never dreamed that it would be the Ukraine, especially given the tough living conditions there.

Edward and I chatted one day about his future, including his plans for getting married and then returning to serve Christ in his native land. "How is Linda feeling about it?" I asked.

With a glow on his face, Edward told me that she is happy and excited about the prospect. Her parents, however, are struggling with the idea of having their daughter go so far away. He added, though, that they had dedicated her to the Lord when she was a baby and were willing to release her to whatever God called her to do with her life.

Those parents have been liberated from the bondage of the earth-side pull of their most precious possession. They would love for their daughter to stay close to them and to see their future grandchildren grow up. But they recognize that those plans are less important than God's eternal cause. When they stand before Christ on that final day, the release and support of their daughter will turn into gold, jewels, and precious stones that are worthy of eternity. In fact, because they gave their daughter to an eternal cause, those jewels may very well be Ukrainian souls won for heaven.

Another possession we can invest in for eternal gain is our financial resources. Jesus commanded us, "Use worldly wealth to gain friends for yourselves, so that when it is gone, you will be welcomed into eternal dwellings" (Luke 16:9 NIV). The heaven-focused believer finds great pleasure in learning to use his funds to enhance and enrich eternity. I like to think of entering heaven's gates as people rush up to introduce themselves to me and tell how money I gave to God was used by Him to guarantee their eternity.

I believe that the life of our Messiah was spared in His infancy because three wise men during a brief visit gave their resources in worship to the King of kings. How else could Mary and Joseph, who were simple, common folk, be able to afford a long journey and residence in Egypt for two years to escape the wrath of a seething Herod who had decreed that all two-year-old boys throughout the land be killed?

Our possessions also include our homes. Russ and Beth Knight bought a small A-frame on the south side of Chicago as well as a piece of vacant land next door. They turned the land into a playground and their home into an after-school shelter for neighborhood kids. Today the playground is safe territory among the gang-ridden turf, and their home is a place where the love of Jesus Christ warmly welcomes city kids, whom they tutor after school. Their home and surrounding land demonstrate the eternal love of Christ to those who know little or nothing of true love, let alone the marvelous embrace of Jesus Christ. There is no doubt in my mind that Russ and Beth are using their home for eternal gain.

Time is an eternal resource. Teaching a Sunday school class can affect the life of a child who may positively affect the lives of others. We can devote our spare time to behind-the-scenes volunteer work, such as offering our skills in writing, nursing, or counseling to clinics in inner-city ministries, or simply stuffing envelopes or changing diapers in a church nursery. This kind of work may offer little recognition at present. But our efforts will surely initiate our heavenly focus and bring eternal gain.

Perception of People

The third result of keeping a heavenward focus is *a new perception of people*. Just before His ascension into heaven, Christ asked His followers to turn their hearts toward the people who did not know Him. He told them to await the Holy Spirit, and then to "be my witnesses in Jerusalem…and to the ends of the earth" (see Acts 1:3–8 NIV). Christ constantly elevated the value of people. And with good reason. People are the only things that will last for eternity.

Everything else stops at the border.

Our perception of people changes from their being commodities to being eternal creatures in need of the redemptive touch of God's grace when we view them through hearts hooked on eternity. We want them to join our pilgrimage and find their way to our eternal home.

If we believe that those around us are candidates for redemption and that we hold the key to their eternity in heaven, we will act and respond with unconditional compassion, generosity, and love. We will no longer see them as objects to be used, abused, manipulated, or consumed for our own pleasure.

A father who looks at his daughter with eternity in view would never abuse her with words that humiliate or anger her, or even consider abusing her physically or sexually, lest he build a wall between her heart and the redemptive work of Jesus Christ. With eternity in focus, business people would act ethically, both because it's right and because it allows them to open the heart-doors of people with whom they work—and even of those against whom they compete.

When our hearts are focused on heaven, crowds at major sporting events and in malls at holiday time become individual people—we begin to care about the eternal destiny of the guy cheering next to us or the rather weird-looking teenagers walking ahead of us. They become the focus of our prayer and compassion rather than a mass of irritating people who elbow their way in front of us.

Perspective on Pain

Fourth, fixing our minds on heaven *changes our perspective on pain.* Christ declared to John in Revelation, "Now the dwelling of God is with men, and he will live with them. They will be his people, and God himself will be with them and be their God. He will wipe every tear from their eyes. There will be no more death or mourning or crying or pain, for the old order of things has passed away…I am making everything new" (Revelation 21:3–5 NIV).

When Joni Eareckson dove into a bay at seventeen and snapped her neck, her life changed drastically. This active teen who loved horseback riding suddenly became paralyzed from the neck down. In the midst of her despair and anger toward God, a friend named Steve Estes turned her heart toward heaven. Joni went through more pain during her rehabilitation, but with eternity waiting, she left the anger and depression and moved on. Today the promise of eternity is evident in her life. She is a blessing to believers and non-believers alike, to the disabled as well as the physically fit. Now married, Joni Eareckson Tada writes books and magazine columns and speaks before large crowds. Heaven often dominates the words she speaks and the pages of her books.

Ken Medema's gifted artistry as singer and songwriter belies the fact that he is blind. On one particular occasion he sat at the keyboard with Joni. "Joni, let me compose a song for us," he requested. As he sang to her of heaven, the notes included these words: "I can't wait to *see* you and have you *dance* in my arms."

African-American slaves were buoyed through the tragic and shameful pain of their plight by their belief in the reality of heaven. In fact, their labor was filled with hymns and spirituals reminding them that a better day was coming.

Whether our present pain is chronic or occasional, physical or emotional, one truth can help us endure: It's all temporary, soon to be replaced by a permanent, pain-free body. Placing our minds on heaven gives us the right perspective on pain.

As Martie and I often said during difficult days of parenting, "This too shall pass." If heaven is in focus, those words ring soothingly at the core of our being.

During his own difficult times, Paul wrote, "I consider that our present sufferings are not worth comparing with the glory that will be revealed in us" (Romans 8:18 NIV). If we think that our reward will be on this side of the grave, we will be easily discouraged and cease to persevere in doing what is right. But if we know that what we do for Him here counts for eternity, though the results may be unseen, we continue to steadfastly carry on for Him regardless of our circumstances (see 1 Corinthians 15:58). A clear view of the other side enables us to persevere on this side.

My first visit to the former Soviet Union was just months after the collapse of the Communist empire. I spoke at churches that were filled with faithful saints. They had persevered through that raging rule of Stalin when they had been relegated to peasant status. Nearly all had been denied education and professional advancement. Yet in spite of seventy years of oppression they filled their churches and sang heartily of their love for God.

As they sang, the interpreter whispered the words to me. Like the African-American slaves, many of their hymns were about heaven. At the close of many services in Russia we stood together and the congregation sang a particular tune that was familiar to me. Though I didn't understand the Russian words, I found myself singing along in English. As they sang, children from the church came with flowers and presented them to us as a farewell gift. During the last chorus my brothers and sisters in that far land lifted their hands and waved farewell to us as they sang:

God be with you till we meet again;
    till we meet,
    till we meet at Jesus' feet;
God be with you till we meet again.

In the midst of their suffering, heaven had become clear and compelling. The song was a sign of heaven in their hearts.

One of the last regimes to fall in Eastern Europe was the government of Romania led by the ruthless dictator Nicolae Ceausescu. The flashpoint of his overthrow occurred when a pastor, Laslo Tökes, refused to obey politically motivated orders to leave his church and take an assignment elsewhere. He stayed inside the church building, and his congregation surrounded the building with their own bodies, creating a human shield against the security forces who sought to take the pastor prisoner.

Most of these Christians did not fear death, even when the soldiers threatened brute force. They were, after all, bound for heaven. What did the temporary loss of life matter? Their courage and faith were too much. The soldiers could not—they would not—challenge these people and their pastor.

This event was the flashpoint that finally led to the toppling of Ceausescu and his regime. Interestingly, the song of the revolution that filled the streets was a hymn of the Romanian church. Its words proclaimed the victory of the second coming of Jesus Christ. It had been their hallmark in dark and terrible days when they were called on to suffer much; and now it would be their victory song as the hope of their freedom dawned.

Throughout the history of the persevering church, courage in times of pain has been grounded in the reality of heaven. When threatened, heaven-focused Christians knew that dying was gain; when their treasures were taken they were not shaken because true treasures are in heaven; when threatened with torture they bore up under it, knowing that the sufferings of this present time are not worthy to be compared with the glory that shall be revealed on the other side.

German theologian Dietrich Bonhoeffer, when he was led to be hung for his commitment to righteousness in the face of Nazi atrocities, confidently spoke these last words: "Oh, God, this is the end; but for me it is just the beginning."

Pleasures on Earth

The fifth outcome of a heavenward focus is *enhanced pleasures on earth.*

When we experience the pleasures that this world offers, they are soon mere memories. Yet, for us who are mindful of heaven, they remind us that the brief pleasures we experience here only foreshadow the fuller, more exhilarating eternal pleasures that await us.

Our earth-side pleasures may include a good meal, a great party, an evening with friends, a good book by the fire, a walk through the country with spring in the air and flowers along the path, or a faithful dog. Clearly, the depth of these pleasures cannot compare to the ongoing pleasure that we will have from His right hand forever. We enjoy pleasures now as merely a foretaste of what is to come.

Our most anticipated pleasures here are often tainted with less-than-expected results.

When Disneyland first opened on July 17, 1955, everyone was excited and wanted to get in. Walt Disney and his staff had sent out invitations to 20,000 special guests—politicians, celebrities, the press, and Disney studio employees. Somehow more than 10,000 uninvited guests were also able to get in with counterfeit passes. By mid-morning, Mickey, Donald, and Goofy were mingling with more that 35,000 children and adults.

Walt called his place the Magic Kingdom, but that first day was anything but magical. When the park opened, cars stretched bumper to bumper for seven miles along the Santa Ana Freeway southeast of Los Angeles. Refreshment stands quickly ran out of supplies. Long lines of cranky visitors formed outside the few operating rest rooms. The Mark Twain steamboat nearly capsized on its maiden voyage. Walt Disney later called the day "Black Sunday."

Now, forty years later, Disneyland has spawned its bigger cousins, Disney World (Orlando), Euro Disney (Paris), and a Tokyo version as well. It has revolutionized amusement parks. And of course, the opening day mistakes were temporary. Disneyland today is a model of order, cleanliness, and fun. It's become almost everything a child could imagine such a place would be.

But at the end of the day, kids and parents go home exhausted, having spent themselves in long lines and crowded rides. The pleasure, as wonderful as it was, is but a memory.

In heaven we will experience "pleasure forever," untainted, unspoiled, and far beyond our expectations.

Purity

The sixth outcome of a mind set on heaven is *a life committed to purity here.* As John notes, "Everyone who has this hope fixed on Him purifies himself, just as He is pure" (1 John 3:3). Recognizing that our souls are eternal, we realize that on earth we are grooming our real selves for heaven. With a mind focused on that eternal union—a final reunion with a God who is absolutely holy and a Savior who is wholly pure and could return at any moment—we feel an urgency to be ready with purity in our hearts.

Every bride wants to be ready for her wedding day. She knows that the best gift she will give the groom is herself—her body, her mind, and her heart—and she wants to be pure and beautiful for him. She spends months preparing for that moment when the organ calls her down the aisle to her husband. She searches for just the right dress and spends hours on her hair and cosmetics. To these add the radiance of her joy, and she appears in unparalleled beauty.

In Jesus' day, the Jewish marriage custom required that the groom go to the bride's father and establish the price for gaining his bride. The father and the future husband sealed the covenant with a cup shared between them. The groom would then leave for a lengthy period, returning to his father's home where he prepared an apartment that would become their home.

Then, without announcement, when everything was finally ready and the wedding feast prepared, he would leave his father's home and walk through the streets of the town to receive his bride and take her home. As he walked, his wedding entourage would shout in the streets, "The bridegroom cometh!" People drawn from their homes would gather in a swelling crowd, shouting the good news. The bride, hearing the shouts from the streets, would meet him at her home and go with him to the feast and to their new home.

Needless to say, there was no time to prepare herself for that great celebration if she waited to hear the shouts in the streets. Given that her hope was fixed on that day, she had already prepared herself in anticipation of his coming for her.

So it is with us whose hearts are fixed on that day, when the trumpet will sound and our bridegroom, the Lord Jesus, will finally come to take us home. Those who live in the context of the reality of that hope live here preparing themselves for there.

When we remember that we will be asked to give an account there for all that we have done here, heaven motivates us to purity.

Sense of Identity

The final outcome of a mind focused on heaven is a transformed sense of identity. Scripture has two identifications for home-bound believers: (1) we are *citizens* of that other land who demonstrate the distinctives of the world to come; and (2) we are *aliens* and *strangers* in this world.

Paul describes us as citizens of heaven in Philippians 1:27–28 and 3:17–21. He tells us as citizens of the celestial city to "conduct yourselves in a manner worthy of the gospel of Christ" (1:27).

Citizens bear the telltale marks of the culture of which they belong. As Christians, we are to bear the identity of the culture of His kingdom which is to come. The kingdom virtues mark us as belonging to heaven just as clearly as my friends from Memphis are marked by their thick southern drawl.

The second proper perception of ourselves is that we don't belong here. We are *aliens* and *strangers* on earth. We may find fulfillment and pleasure along the way, but we're just passing through. Let's say your destination for a summer vacation is the Grand Canyon. You may be able to enjoy the trip, with a smooth ride and new sights along the way, but your focus is on that final destination. All you do and the decisions you make along the way are determined by that destination. That, after all, is where you belong at a certain time. Everything else is interesting but secondary to arriving at the rim of the canyon, looking across the chasm and down on the Colorado River and exclaiming, "I'm finally here! What a view! It was worth the trip."

Scripture deals with this issue of belonging through several word pictures. No longer strangers and aliens toward God, we are now strangers, aliens, and exiles of this earth.[5] These are pilgrim words that indicate, as one scholar put it, "someone who lives for a short while in a foreign place."[6] *Strangers* have no long-term ties; they are in transit. Their lives stand out by the distinct differences of the culture to which they belong.

Aliens have a unique perspective of possessions. Although they may own things along the way, all these things become dispensable in light of their destination. They recognize that ownership is temporary, so they hold things loosely and share them with those in need (1 Timothy 6:18). Their possessions become instruments of fairness and righteousness (Leviticus 25:23). King David, a man of great wealth, reflected on his pilgrimage in a prayer of thanksgiving before God, noting,

> Wealth and honor come from you; you are the ruler of all things. In your hands are strength and power to exalt and give strength to all. Now, our God, we give you thanks, and praise your glorious name. But who am I, and who are my people, that we should be able to give as generously as this? Everything comes from you, and we have given you only what comes from your hand. We are aliens and strangers in your sight, as were all our forefathers. Our days on earth are like a shadow, without hope. O Lord our God, as for all this abundance that we have provided for building you a temple for your Holy Name, it comes from your hand, and all of it belongs to you. (1 Chronicles 29:12–16 NIV)

The pilgrim mind-set, best exemplified by Abraham (see Hebrews 11:8–10), recognizes that as aliens we don't belong here and that we live seeking the country to which we do belong.[7]

To claim a pilgrim's identity means that we always know we're not home yet. For us the best is yet to come. Therefore, everything is expendable here, free to be used for the glory and gain of the King.

Living in the reality of heaven has tremendous relevance. When we envision heaven as our home, everything in life is radically rearranged. It affects our posture toward God, our possessions, people, pain, and pleasure. And heaven in our hearts purifies us and alters our sense of identity.

If we say we believe in heaven, then let's show our redemptive passport. Let's look at the ledger of our checkbooks and the pages of our Day-Timers.® Do we see heaven in how we view and treat people? Is there peace in the midst of pain? Do earthly pleasures stimulate our hearts toward a thirst for pleasures forevermore? Let's check the purity of our souls and our identity as pilgrims rather than permanent residents.

When heaven is the habit of our hearts we love more freely, worship more deeply, share more gladly, and suffer and sacrifice more readily. When the other side is real, everything on this side is radically, wonderfully rearranged.

What then does it take to make heaven a habit of our hearts?

1. C. S. Lewis, *Mere Christianity* (New York: Macmillan, 1943), 118.

2. Ibid., 119.

3. Dan McGraw, "The Christian Capitalists," *U.S. News and World Report*, 13 March 1995, 53.

4. Francis A. Schaeffer, *No Little People* (Downers Grove, Ill.: InterVarsity, 1974), 258–71.

5. Ephesians 2:19; Hebrews 11:13; 1 Peter 2:11.

6. H. Bietenhard, "*Parepidemos*," *Dictionary of New Testament Theology* (Grand Rapids, Mich.: Zondervan, 1975), 1:690.

7. Six characteristics of the pilgrim mind-set can be found by studying Hebrews 11:13–19. Briefly, the passage shows that as pilgrims: (1) we live here believing God's promises will be fulfilled ultimately in the world to come (v. 13); (2) we readily sense we don't belong on earth, and are seeking the world to come (v.13); (3) though we could choose to return and live in the earthbound environment from which we were called, we refuse to think backward to what is past (v.15); (4) we believe nothing here compares to the better country to which we are going, so our affections are set there (v.15); (5) with our affections on eternity, God is not ashamed to be called our God (v.15); (6) nothing here is of greater value than our relationship with God, therefore we can be obedient to the point of ultimate sacrifice (vv. 17–19).

ACKNOWLEDGMENTS

"The Scriptures Anticipate His Coming" originally published as "His Coming Is Sure…Are You?" in *Growing Deep in the Christian Life* by Charles Swindoll. © 1986, 1995 by Charles R. Swindoll, Inc. Used by permission of Zondervan Publishing House. All rights reserved.

"The Troubling Trends Portray His Coming" originally published as "Signs of the Times" in *Storm Warning* by Billy Graham. © 1992 by Billy Graham. Used by permission of Word Publishing, Nashville, Tenn. All rights reserved.

"The Prophets Promised His Coming" by Stanley Ellisen. © 1998 by Stanley Ellisen. Used by permission of the author. All rights reserved.

"The Psalms Include His Coming" originally published as "Prophecy and Psalms" in *Rediscovering Prophecy* by Ronald Allen. © 1983. Used by permission of the author. All rights reserved.

"The Promises to Israel Predict His Coming" originally published as "Prophecy of the Future of Israel as a Nation" in *Major Bible Prophecies* by John F. Walvoord. © 1991 by John F. Walvoord. Used by permission of Zondervan Publishing House. All rights reserved.

"The Alignment of Nations Suggests His Coming" originally published as "The Alignment of Nations and Christ's Coming" in *Will Man Survive?* by J. Dwight Pentecost. © 1971. Used by permission of the author. All rights reserved.

"The Condition of the Church Indicates His Coming" originally

Printed in the United States
by Baker & Taylor Publisher Services